# Beyond Article 19

## Libraries and Social and Cultural Rights

# Beyond Article 19

Libraries and Social and Cultural Rights

Edited by Julie Biando Edwards
and Stephan P. Edwards

Foreword by Toni Samek

Library Juice Press
Duluth, Minnesota

Published by Litwin Books, LLC, 2010
PO Box 3320
Duluth, MN 55803

http://litwinbooks.com/

This book is printed on acid-free paper that meets all present ANSI standards for archival preservation.

Library of Congress Cataloging-in-Publication Data

Beyond Article 19 : libraries and social and cultural rights / edited by Julie Biando Edwards and Stephan P. Edwards ; foreword by Toni Samek.
        p. cm.
Includes bibliographical references and index.
ISBN 978-1-936117-19-2 (acid-free paper)
1. Libraries and society. 2. Libraries and community. 3. Library science--Moral and ethical aspects. 4. Librarians--Professional ethics. 5. Multiculturalism. 6. Cultural property--Protection. 7. United Nations. General Assembly. Universal Declaration of Human Rights. I. Edwards, Julie Biando. II. Edwards, Stephan P. III. United Nations. General Assembly. Universal Declaration of Human Rights.
        Z716.4B428 2010
        021.2--dc22
                        2010037149

# Contents

# Foreword

## By Toni Samek

This monograph comprises a set of critical librarianship essays that collectively suggest a significant suite of lessons about the library as an important means to self-determination for all peoples in the face of global market fundamentalism. The primary lesson communicated in this book is the importance of considering the inherent relationships between the Universal Declaration of Human Rights (UDHR) and related covenants, library diversity and inclusion statements, and other positions taken by library and information organizations as sets and super-sets of persuasion and consensus building – some arguably optimistic and others more threatening. (The catch is that you can only do so when and if you can access the positions in the appropriate language/s to begin with.) In reading this book, one can learn about how these ideological assertions reflect the inevitable tensions that exist between individual rights and community traditions, standards, and values. And the related lessons gathered are many; most suggesting that the most viable and authentic solutions to the cultural problems we face now will come in time and through multiple human engagements and interruptions, not as quick fixes or techno-managerial efficiencies.

The gentle, yet in some instances haunting, musings captured in this book braid discussions of the cultural record, community and communities, tribes, culture, tolerance, colonialism, morality, identity, collectivity, western modalities, heritage, cultural life, language, universalism, globalization, migration, and pluralism. The book also offers probing of the taxonomies of special groups and prods at ubiquitous and unfortunate reductive, negating, and racialized treatments of "minority," marginalized, and underrepresented parties. Human rights, moral dilemmas, international law, the state, communication, multicultural landscapes, and new immigrant patterns are reoccurring themes that bring the UDHR specific articles 3, 7, 12, 15, 19 - and especially 27 – into play and replay. It is advantageous to read this book with the UDHR in plain view (quite literally). In showing how human rights are interdependent, indivisible – and in some cases transversal – the authors guide the reader. For example, one contributor helps us to look underneath the cover of culture to find bare and exposed specific freedoms (e.g., religion, food habits, rituals, language, and performance art). Cautioned about the liberalization of and de-territorialization of markets that have grown with globalization, the book exposes numerous examples of the ongoing lack of understanding about orality and literacy and about status quo and dominant cultures of information exchange that serve to perpetuate misunderstandings about various contributors to traditional knowledge and knowledge activism (e.g., elders, priests, midwives, storytellers, and oral historians), including within library teachings. In discussion of the politics of library development in Sub-Saharan Africa and related cases, which introduce vital discussions about indigenous ways of being and knowing, the reader is placed at a distance from Anglo-American culturally situated codes of librarianship. In this sense, this book represents a conscious engagement in the ethics of collective knowledge, including its naming and other aspects of its organization.

In this volume, the journey in ideas extends across and through the sub-communities of librarianship into the broader cultural networks. Whether you are a storyteller, archivist, documentalist, or national librarian, and so on, there is something in this book that will set you thinking about life, liberty, and the law; justice and injustice; information, misinformation, disinformation, and propaganda; education, knowledge, and power; equality, equity, and universal access to information; and how library workers, administrators, educators, students, activists, and their stakeholders consciously and unconsciously enable these words for better and for worse.

Library communities have responsibilities to the past, present, and future, because library rhetoric and reality participates in intentional, unintentional, and systemic imposition of burdens, obligations, and disadvantages on individuals and classes of individuals. I extend thanks to the book's editors (Julie Biando Edwards and Stephan Edwards), authors (Julie Biando Edwards, Frans Albarillo, Natalia Taylor Poppeliers, Loriene Roy, and Kristen Hogan), and publisher (Rory Litwin) for their collective intelligence and formidable creative expression about library labour and the human condition. Together these teachers and learners make a stark case for global library citizenship. And this is welcome in an era in which germ warfare, nuclear armament, food and water shortages, natural disasters, human-designed destruction, homelessness, and war crimes beg new understandings of how to advocate and practice peace, spiritual well-being, and sustainability on a planet shared by sentient beings. But these cultural workers are part a minority of their own field's making. They are far outnumbered by bureaucratized, corporatized, and militarized library and information workforces and discourses. And I am left pondering the weight of library complacency, which will undoubtedly limit the place of this book in reading lists and on library shelves. (I know of only one graduate library course deliberately dedicated to the subject of libraries and human rights, one developed and taught by the pioneering educator Kathleen de la Peña McCook at the University of South Florida entitled Libraries and Human Rights: A Seminar). A tangible burden falls to the readers of this book, as they may choose action or inaction in regards to the ideas presented.

Toni Samek
*Bayswater, Nova Scotia*
*20 July 2010*
*writing freely in English on a laptop in the sunlight*

# Acknowledgments

This book is about community, and it has taken a community to produce it. We'd like to thank the following people for the many ways in which they have contributed to the process of creating this collection:

Thanks to colleagues at the Peabody Institute Library in Peabody, Massachusetts. Under the direction of Martha Holden, the Peabody Library is an example of the ways in which a library can truly be responsive to the community in which it is situated. Working with you was my formative experience as a librarian and is an inspiration still.

Thanks to Kelley Rae Unger and Melissa Rauseo – dear friends and librarians extraordinaire, community champions, pillars of unfailing support, and our lifeline back to public libraries.

Thanks to Sue Samson – thoughtful early reader and mentor. Your willingness to share your experience and advice has made this process much easier, and your genuine excitement on our behalf has made this process much more fun.

Thanks to Nupur Sen – reader, scholar, and friend.

Thanks to Professor Paul Lauren – our teacher.

Editing a book is a bit like being a shepherd; it requires coaxing chapters into shape while recognizing and respecting the autonomy and vision of the individual authors. Thanks to the contributors to this book, each of whom took up the topic of libraries and cultural rights and crafted it into something beyond what we would have ever expected. Watching the ideas form was wonderful and seeing the ways in which the chapters connected was gratifying. It has been a pleasure to work with you and a privilege to share in your ideas from beginning to end.

Thanks to Toni Samek for blazing the trail, and for her contribution to this book in the form of the foreword; thanks also to all librarians dedicated to human rights, critical practice, and an examination of our profession.

Thanks to Rory Litwin and Library Juice for their devotion to publishing works of critical and radical librarianship and to thus giving voice to a small but passionate slice of the profession.

Finally, most importantly, thanks to our families, especially our parents – Steve and Linda Biando and William and Stephanie Edwards – for their constant love and support. They are the rocks upon which we build. *Sempre famiglia*.

# Introduction

When the Universal Declaration of Human Rights (UDHR) was written in 1948, the drafters made sure to include cultural rights in the final document, "placing them on the same level as civil and political [individual] rights."[1] All of the rights outlined in the UDHR are, as Elsa Stamatopoulou writes, "interdependent and indivisible,"[2] which means that group rights–including cultural rights–are no less important than individual rights. Given this, it should follow that librarianship, as a profession concerned with the individual rights of access, inquiry, and speech, should thus also be concerned with cultural rights. If all rights are related, moving beyond individual rights to consider how to incorporate cultural rights into the profession is a new and exciting prospect.

The purpose of this book is to explore the ways in which librarians can think about and incorporate aspects of human rights into their professional practice and philosophy. In the summer of 2008, we began thinking about how libraries and cultural rights intersect. What are cultural rights? What do cultural rights mean for libraries? What can librarians do to promote cultural rights? The book you are now holding is the result of those questions. This collection of essays is an exploratory project. Written, by-and-large, by librarians and for librarians, the following chapters examine the ways in which cultural rights can inform library practice and philosophy. It is important to approach the book from the perspective

---

[1] Paul Gordon Lauren, *The Evolution of International Human Rights: Visions Seen* (Philadelphia: University of Pennsylvania Press, 1998), 236.

[2] Elsa Stamatopoulou, Cultural Rights in International Law: Article 27 of the Universal Declaration of Human Rights and Beyond (Leiden, The Netherlands: Martinus Nijhoff Publishers, 2007), 143.

of librarianship–this is not a work of human rights scholarship. Rather, it is a book about librarianship, using human rights (particularly cultural rights) as a lens through which we might consider our work in new ways.

Each of the essays presented here examines cultural rights and libraries using the specific language of Article 27 of the UDHR, which establishes the right freely to participate in the cultural life of the community and is one of several articles dealing with cultural rights. Janusz Symonides argues that cultural rights are a "neglected category of human rights,"[3] and this collection attempts to address that, at least within the profession of librarianship. The essays that follow explore the relationship between libraries and Article 27 in a variety of ways and encourage readers to consider librarianship in the context of group rights, not just individual rights. The book, which suggests looking beyond the individual rights of opinion, expression, and inquiry as codified in Article 19 and towards the rights codified in Article 27, is philosophical and theoretical in scope. In the first essay, I focus on the symbolic possibilities of libraries and argue that libraries are the institutions best capable of embodying the right to participate in the cultural life of the community. Frans Albarillo argues for a consideration of language rights as group rights and asserts that libraries must adjust their philosophies of practice in order to promote cultural rights through the support of language rights. Natalia Taylor Poppeliers explores the development and evolution of library services in Sub-Saharan Africa and questions whether or not current rhetoric and practice engages and aligns with the principles set forth in Article 27. Finally, Loriene Roy and Kristen Hogan close out the collection with their examination of library services and indigenous rights, uncovering both the strengths and the weaknesses of Article 27 in addressing the rights of indigenous peoples.

This is a broad collection, and each essay is different in both its philosophy and approach. At the center of all, though, is Article 27,

---

[3] Janusz Symonides, "Cultural Rights: A Neglected Category of Human Rights," *International Social Science Journal* 50:158 (December 1998): 559.

and together these essays provide a starting point for thinking about libraries, community, and cultural rights. As you will see, not all of the essays necessarily agree on the definitions of cultural and group rights, or on the best ways to implement those rights. Rather than seeing this as a problem, however, we embrace it as an example of the complexity of these topics and encourage readers to consider what these different interpretations mean for themselves, for their communities, for the profession, and for library services. The intention of this collection is to look at and think about cultural rights and their place in librarianship. It is absolutely essential to note, however, that while this book advocates for an exploration of librarianship beyond Article 19, we understand that a focus on promoting, protecting, and supporting the right to freely participate in the cultural life of the community may be a luxury for many librarians. Librarians in the United States and across the world deal daily with issues of privacy, censorship, government filtering or government monitoring. There are libraries that are underfunded and ill equipped. There are places around the globe where issues of free access and inquiry and expression take precedence over cultural rights. These violations of human rights are immediately pressing, and this collection in no way diminishes or ignores the challenges that many librarians, their patrons, and their communities face each day. Wherever such injustice exists, the struggle for basic human rights must never be abandoned. I do believe, though, that for librarians who are fortunate enough to be able to look beyond Article 19, there is room to start thinking about cultural rights and community life. This collection will hopefully provide some initial insights.

The UDHR is an imperfect tool, to be sure–it neglects to explicitly mention the rights of minorities and indigenous peoples, for example. It is best read in conjunction with its sister documents, the International Covenant on Civil and Political Rights and the International Covenant on Economic, Social, and Cultural Rights, and it is better understood through the many international declarations and covenants which have followed in the years since 1948. However imperfect a tool, though, it is a tool nonetheless. The UDHR does provide a way for librarians to "plug into" human rights, so to speak. It provides a foundation from which to think about and develop services and policies. Often, when talking or thinking about human rights, it is easy to think about what has gone wrong–what is going wrong–in the world. Human rights violations are real. Sometimes, though, it is as useful to think about where we can succeed as it is to acknowledge where we fail; it is as important to consider not only what is wrong, but what could be right.

Though the UDHR has holes, it is also holistic, as indicated earlier by Stamatopoulou. Despite the intended indivisibility of the articles in the UDHR, however, some do prove to be more pertinent to librarians than others. Recently, librarians, authors, and activists have been writing more on libraries and human rights. Toni Samek and Kathleen de la Peña McCook and Katharine Phenix have all highlighted some of the articles in the UDHR that are more germane to librarians, including Articles 3, 7, 12, and 27, among others.[4] This is the first collection, to our knowledge, that intentionally looks at Article 27 (or any other article) and its relation to librarianship. This collection, though the first in English on this subject, will hopefully not be the last. It is our hope that librarians, authors, and activists will consider cultural rights in ways that we cannot yet imagine. The work presented in this collection is just the start–eventually we'd love to see an entire series of books exploring the relationship between libraries and the various articles that most pertain to the profession.

---

[4] See Toni Samek, *Librarianship and Human Rights: A Twenty-First Century Guide* (Oxford: Chandos, 2007); Toni Samek and Kevin Rioux, "Apologies, Boycotts & Law Reform: Why and How Library and Information Workers Talk and Walk Human Rights" in *Proceedings of the International Conference on Libraries from a Human Rights Perspective, 31 March – 2 April, 2008,* ed. Nabil Alawi (Ramallah, Palestine: Ramallah Center for Human Rights Studies, 2008): 84-97, and Kathleen de la Peña McCook and Katherine J. Phenix, "Human Rights, Democracy and Librarians," in *The Portable MLIS: Insights from the Experts,* ed. Ken Haycock and Brooke Sheldon (Santa Barbara, CA: Libraries Unlimited, 2008).

As with any book, this one has limitations. An author can only write from his or her own perspective–his or her individual place in the world and in history. I write from my own place and perspective–that of a white woman with experience in rural and urban public libraries, in primarily English-speaking (though ethnically and racially diverse) communities. The authors represented here write from their own perspectives as well, and the perspectives are broad and varied. While the essays here explore both international and indigenous issues, the majority of the sources consulted are in English. And, while there is no doubt that much more can be written about Article 27 and libraries, in the meantime we hope that this book will spark or expand the interest of librarians concerned with issues of culture and community.

All books are acts of optimism, and I am optimistic that this collection will generate further inquiry and writing, and that librarians will embrace an obligation not only to individual and cultural rights, but to human rights of all kinds. Paul Gordon Lauren has written that human rights are born first out of the visions of "men and women who possess a capacity to go beyond the confines of what is or what has been, and to creatively dream or imagine what might be."[5] I see no reason why librarians cannot be amongst those men and women.

*Julie Biando Edwards ~ Missoula, Montana*
*July 21, 2010*

---

[5] Lauren, The Evolution of International Human Rights, 1.

# Symbolic Possibilities

Julie Biando Edwards

*"We in librarianship stick so carefully to the first amendment issues that we don't realize that we need a broader way of looking at the right thing to do."*
~ *Kathleen de la Peña McCook*[1]

The problem is so deceptively simple. When Serbian firebombs destroyed the National and University Library of Sarajevo, a strong symbol of Bosnian multiculturalism, the international community reacted with outrage. When looters burned and ravaged the Iraq National Library and Archive in 2003, and when the United States military later commandeered it as a temporary strategic base from which to counteract the insurgency, the world was similarly appalled. Such cases drew public ire for a variety of reasons, not the least of which being that the materials housed in these institutions were rare and unique – priceless, centuries old, and fundamentally irreplaceable. The global condemnation of what would come to be termed *libricide* is not difficult to understand.[2] In each case, in a matter of days, significant portions of national and world heritage were targeted in acts of war and reduced to ashes and rubble. Indeed, for someone to witness the destruction of these libraries –

---

[1] Kathleen de la Peña McCook, "Human Rights: A New Model of Librarianship," audio recording. http://iminervapodcast.blogspot.com/2009/02/dr-kathleen-de-la-pena-mccook-interview_12.html (accessed 21 July 2009).
[2] Rebecca Knuth, *Libricide: The Regime Sponsored Destruction of Books and Libraries in the Twentieth Century* (Westport, CT: Praeger Publications, 2003).

and the valiant, seemingly quixotic attempts of librarians, intellectuals and citizens to rescue what they could of their written heritage – and not be moved seems nearly incomprehensible.

But these are special cases, no? These national libraries and archives are home to the treasures of a nation. By definition these institutions are unique, and communities set them apart as places in which to house and preserve the best and rarest books, maps, manuscripts, documents and records as a testimony to the history of a place and people. To lose one of these institutions is to lose material that exists nowhere else in the world. The destruction of institutions such as these is a blow to world heritage and rightly is of grave concern to those of us who serve in a profession dedicated to the preservation and dissemination of information. To lose the materials in these libraries and archives is to erase the possibility that future researchers, scholars and citizens will have access to the written records of the past.

Recently, I have spent time writing and thinking about the destruction of these two specific institutions.[3] My thinking, though, has focused less on the materials than on the symbolism of destroyed libraries and on what that destruction means for the communities that claim these libraries. In this way, then, I have found myself a bit far afield of the thinking of many librarians who, by professional training, are rightly concerned with what the destruction of materials means for future access, research, and scholarship. In some ways, I am approaching the problem from a different angle and arriving at the same conclusion – any act of libricide is a terrible blow to a community and is fundamentally opposed to the principles of librarianship. On this there is likely to be little disagreement. Where the divergence in thinking occurs is in where

---

[3] Julie Biando Edwards and Stephan P. Edwards, "Culture and the New Iraq: The Iraq National Library and Archive, 'Imagined Community,' and the Future of the Iraqi Nation," *Libraries and the Cultural Record* 43:3 (2008): 327-342; Julie Biando Edwards and Stephan P. Edwards, "Libraries, Cultural Life, and Community Identity," in *Proceedings of the International Conference on Libraries from a Human Rights Perspective, 31 March – 2 April, 2008*, ed. Nabil Alawi (Ramallah, Palestine: Ramallah Center for Human Rights Studies, 2008): 72-83.

one chooses to put the focus of the destruction – on the materials themselves or on their relationship to the psyche of the community.

This leads me back to that deceptively simple problem. The assertion, posed to me by numerous colleagues, is paraphrased thus: "The loss of the National and University Library of Sarajevo and the Iraq National Library and Archive is devastating. Similarly, the loss of our National Archives or Library of Congress would be devastating on the same scale. But surely these libraries are in a different class. And surely, while no one wants to see any library burned or otherwise destroyed, with the advent of approval plans, library consortia, corporate databases, electronic books, and the digitization of rare and archival materials, the loss incurred by the destruction of most libraries – particularly in the industrialized world – would be much mitigated." This was the problem presented to me, and it is with this problem that I lay the foundations for this chapter.

In the strictest sense, the sentiments expressed here are correct. In most average public or small university libraries today the material losses incurred would indeed be minimal. All of the advances mentioned above – particularly the ubiquity of databases, the growing emphasis on digitization, and the acquisition of electronic books – means that relatively large percentages of library collections are either replaceable or preserved in formats other than print. Taken to the logical conclusion, one could argue that the destruction of many physical libraries doesn't represent a significant loss of material at all because the virtual library would remain (theoretically) untouched and intact. Someone more cynical may go on to argue that the loss of physical books, particularly in a public library, is not necessarily cause for great concern because, as most of these books are for popular and recreational reading, they are easily replaced and they don't represent the apex of culture or heritage that the materials in a national library or archive do.

These are all logical and pragmatic arguments and they honestly and rationally point to the ways in which the library has evolved and is situated in the twenty-first century. They are not without a measure of truth, which is why they gave me initial pause and

prompted me to embark on the writing of this chapter. Upon reflection, I realized that such a line of reasoning was completely
consistent with the traditional perspectives of the profession. The
emphasis is on materials, preservation, efficiency and the sharing of
resources, all of which ultimately serve to provide access to individuals. This has been the focus of librarianship since its inception
and, though there have been different iterations of this model, the
fact is that a library is nothing if it cannot provide access to materials for its patrons.

But while this is indeed the foundation of librarianship, I would
argue that this emphasis on materials, and on their evolving creation, storage, preservation, and retrieval, misses a larger point. I
posit a question: "Are libraries *only* the sum of their materials? Is a
library *only* important insofar as it can provide access to information?" These questions may seem to be in direct conflict with the
statement above that libraries are nothing if they cannot provide
access to materials. But is that *all* they do? Is that even the most
important thing they do? Is there no larger purpose, no greater
meaning to the library – any library – as an institution? Should we
privilege national and university archives over other libraries simply
because of the uniqueness of their materials? Or should we consider instead shifting the paradigm from one in which materials are
of primary importance – because they educate, entertain and enlighten individual users or because they are rare, sacred or priceless
– to one in which we philosophically reconsider the library as more
than the sum of its collections, more than merely a place to get
information?

There is no doubt that materials are important and it is true that
today, as collections become more and more homogenous, most
library holdings are not unique. But to focus exclusively, or even
primarily, on materials and information is to miss the ways in
which libraries can continue to evolve in the twenty-first century.
We have, as a profession, for so long privileged our collections
over our communities even while passionately asserting that the
collections exist to serve our patrons. We have laudably advocated
for free inquiry and expression and for the privacy rights of our
patrons, codifying these principles in our bills of rights and codes

of ethics. We have been in library boardrooms and in courtrooms arguing for the right of any patron to access and read any material and to then do with that material what he will, forgetting that we, and the individuals we serve, do not exist in vacuums. We have been so committed to privacy rights, to individual access, and to our role as the ultimate information providers that we neglect the bigger picture. As I have noted in previous work, "[d]espite the strong tradition of advocating for individual rights, librarians have not been encouraged to, or perhaps have simply never imagined that they can, consider the work that they do within a larger context."[4] In our refusal to see ourselves as more than the sum of our parts, and in our ever increasing focus on the ways in which technology is changing how we and our patrons interact with those parts, we are missing an opportunity to look at how our libraries serve our communities, how they reflect culture, how they promote and shape culture and how we can hold on to a place of meaning, and *be* a place of meaning, in the ceaseless information revolution. We need to consider what those materials do, not just what they are. And we need to consider what they do for communities, not just for individuals. Ultimately, I think that we need to lay those materials aside and start to consider the symbolic possibilities of libraries.

*          *          *

Symbolism can be a tricky word. It is slippery, and much less concrete a concept than "library materials" or even "information." What does it mean for a library to be symbolic? What are the symbolic possibilities that can arise out of our institutions? Libraries have, in fact, always been symbolic – of democracy, of the individual desire to better oneself, of egalitarianism, and of an enlightened, cultured and free society. At the same time, if we are to be honest, we must recognize that libraries, in specific times and places, in our country and elsewhere, have been seen as symbols of elitism, imperialism and colonialism. The idea of assigning libraries a meaning

---

[4] Edwards and Edwards, "Libraries, Cultural Life, and Community Identity," 75.

beyond that of information provider is not new. What is relatively new is thinking about libraries as symbolic of the communities in which they are situated and in which they serve. To conceive of libraries in this way is to imagine them not as static repositories but as organic and dynamic agents of culture – reflecting and shaping the communities that claim them. This has been the guiding principle in my research, and to conceive of libraries in this way is to realize that the destruction of a library, any library, is not so much about the destruction of materials as it is about the destruction of the fabric of a people and a place. As Rebecca Knuth notes in her seminal work, *Libricide*, the contents of a library do not stand alone but are rather inextricably linked to group identity and culture. She concludes her chapter on the cultural evolution and functions of libraries by stating that "whatever the defining identity of a group, the destruction of its libraries impedes the cultural development the group as a whole, diminishes quality of life, and damages the self-esteem of group members. It also compromises, on many levels, the group's future."[5]

Establishing libraries as symbolic of the communities in which they serve is only the first step, however. My larger aim, and the one that is more important, more pressing, and more in keeping with the goals of this collection, is to explicitly establish libraries – particularly public libraries in the United States – as symbolic of the principles set forth in the Universal Declaration of Human Rights (UDHR). In recent years there has been an increased focus, particularly among those in the profession interested in critical librarianship, on aligning libraries, librarians and library services with human rights principles. Authors, educators, and activists such as Toni Samek and Kathleen de la Peña McCook and Katharine Phenix have written persuasively about the need to situate librarianship more firmly into the larger human rights discourse.[6] Both

---

[5] Knuth, *Libricide*, 45.

[6] See Toni Samek, *Librarianship and Human Rights: A Twenty-First Century Guide* (Oxford: Chandos, 2007); Toni Samek and Kevin Rioux, "Apologies, Boycotts & Law Reform: Why and How Library and Information Workers Talk and Walk Human Rights" in *Proceedings of the International Conference on Libraries from a Human Rights Perspective, 31 March – 2 April,*

the American Library Association (ALA) and the International Federation of Library Associations (IFLA) have drawn upon the language in the UDHR in the creation of their own documents.[7] However, despite the recognition of the importance of human rights to librarianship as evidenced by the adoption of language by ALA and IFLA, and despite the efforts of Samek, McCook and Phenix, and others, the profession as a whole has paid relatively little attention to issues of human rights beyond Article 19 of the UDHR, which states,

*2008*, ed. Nabil Alawi (Ramallah, Palestine: Ramallah Center for Human Rights Studies, 2008): 84-97; Toni Samek, "An Introduction to Librarianship for Human Rights," in *Educating for Human Rights and Global Citizenship*, ed. Ali A. Abdi and Lynette Shultz (Albany, NY: State University of New York Press, 2008): 205-222; Kathleen de la Peña McCook and Katherine J. Phenix, "Human Rights and Librarianship," *Reference and User Services Quarterly* 45:1 (2005): 23-26; Kathleen de la Peña McCook and Katherine J. Phenix, "Public Libraries and Human Rights," *Public Library Quarterly* 25 (2006): 57-73; Kathleen de la Peña McCook and Katherine J. Phenix, "Human Rights, Democracy and Librarians," in *The Portable MLIS: Insights from the Experts*, ed. Ken Haycock and Brooke Sheldon (Santa Barbara, CA: Libraries Unlimited, 2008). For complete bibliographies of these authors, please see http://www.ualberta.ca/~asamek/writings.htm and http://shell.cas.usf.edu/mccook/selectedpublications.htm.

[7] See the ALA Policy Manual, Section 58, International Relations, (http://www.ala.org/ala/aboutala/governance/policymanual/internation al.cfm); the ALA Resolution on IFLA, Human Rights, and Freedom of Expression (http://www.ala.org/ala/aboutala/offices/iro/ awardsactivities/resolutionifla.cfm); the IFLA Statutes, Article 2, (http://www.ifla.org/en/statutes); the ALA Privacy Toolkit (http://www.ala.org/ala/aboutala/offices/oif/iftoolkits/toolkitsprivacy/i ntroduction/introduction.cfm); and the IFLA Internet Manifesto (http://www.ifla.org/en/publications/the-ifla-internet-manifesto) for examples.

*Everyone has the right to freedom of opinion and expression; this right includes freedom to hold opinions without interference and to seek, receive, and impart information and ideas through any media and regardless of frontiers.[8]*

As recently as 2009, McCook declared that the "Universal Declaration of Human Rights [provides] the model that we need in librarianship" and predicted that "librarians in the twenty-first century are going to gradually adopt a comprehensive human rights perspective."[9] It is in a spirit of agreement and solidarity that I take up this challenge and enter the conversation to assert that libraries, in being symbolic of the communities in which they are situated, are also symbolic of human rights beyond those set out in Article 19. I will argue specifically that libraries are symbolic of the principles set forth in the first paragraph of Article 27 of the UDHR, which states,

*Everyone has the right freely to participate in the cultural life of the community, to enjoy the arts, and to share in scientific advancement and its benefits.[10]*

Without rejecting the principles set forth in Article 19, we must look towards Article 27 if we are to really use the UDHR as the new model for librarianship. I contend that libraries are symbolic of the communities in which they serve and that this symbolism must extend into the realm of human rights discourse and practice in order to move librarianship into the twenty-first century. Because I believe that using the UDHR as the new model of librarianship will provide the best and most innovative way for librarians to both conceptualize and put into practice new modes of thinking and responding to our patrons, I assert that looking beyond Article 19 to focus on Article 27 is the step that the profession should next take in the establishment of this new model. Indeed, given the complexities of the terms "community" and "culture," and given the contentiousness with which these terms can be met in our increasingly globalized world, I maintain that libraries are perhaps the

---

[8] United Nations, *Universal Declaration of Human Rights.*
http://www.un.org/en/documents/udhr/ (accessed 9 September 2009).
[9] de la Peña McCook, "Human Rights: A New Model of Librarianship."
[10] United Nations, *Universal Declaration of Human Rights.*

*only* public institution that can proactively embody the rights set forth in Article 27.

## Rethinking Our Role in Communities

There has been no shortage of material written on libraries and community life.[11] However, none of the numerous articles, chapters, and books published has explicitly linked the library's role in a community with the principles set forth in Article 27. That is, the current literature has by and large not connected libraries, community, and human rights in a way that allows us to conceptualize our role in reflecting and creating the cultural life of the community as human rights work. What this body of literature has done, however, is examine how libraries interact with, serve and advocate for the people of a community – to return library services, in a sense, to their most essential emphasis.

McCook, in her book on libraries and community, *A Place at the Table: Participating in Community Building,* establishes the prominent role that libraries can – indeed, must – play in community life. She early on tackles the complex nature of the term "community" by stating that

> [i]n libraries we speak of community quite broadly to indicate all whom we are mandated to serve. Where once this meant fairly precise taxing districts, libraries have, through interlocal agreements, reciprocal borrowing, interlibrary loan, and cyber access, extended our service bases. Thus, to librarians, "building community" might mean extension to people beyond governmental jurisdictions, but more often than not in the broader literature, the term seems to mean the geographic boundaries of taxed service or smaller neighborhood areas.[12]

For my purposes I will consider community in a broader sense, "beyond government jurisdictions," and loosely use Benedict An-

---

[11] David Carr, *A Place Not a Place: Reflection and Possibility in Museums and Libraries* (Oxford: AltaMira Press, 2006); Kathleen de la Peña McCook, *A Place at the Table: Participating in Community Building* (Chicago: ALA Editions, 2000); Robert Putnam, *Better Together: Restoring the American Community* (New York: Simon and Schuster, 2003).
[12] de la Pena McCook, *A Place at the Table*, 6.

derson's idea of "imagined community" as a place from which to begin thinking about community in a different way. Although Anderson's work deals with issues of the nation, nationalism and print capitalism and although he writes of an "imagined political community" [13] I have used his concept in the past and maintain still that "community [can exist] primarily in the mind [and] is a dynamic entity that can incorporate all kinds of individuals with different and often competing interests and [can] cut across traditional boundaries of identity."[14] This definition applies, I think, beyond the nation. I would argue that it is a useful working definition for community as I envision it in this chapter – as an amalgamation of individuals who together form a group, however imperfect and messy.

Though governmental and geographical boundaries do define our municipalities (a fact that is important when considering public library funding in particular), I think of community as something more organic, having less to do with laws than with lives. Considering community in this way allows room to focus on both the individuals and groups that come together to make their lives in a certain place. In this sense, the community is made up of people and is thus dynamic, shifting, swelling and shrinking. Community is a living thing in this model – an entity not bound by borders but defined as the actual groups within those borders. Such a definition demands that social institutions, chief among them libraries, work continuously to understand and serve the community. Libraries in particular, in this case, have the opportunity to become a place that reflects the community back on itself and have the opportunity to shape the cultural life of the community in a way that supports the needs and rights of all of the groups that make up the community.

Perhaps one of the most important pieces on libraries and community published in recent years comes not from a librarian at all but from a public policy expert. Robert Putnam devotes an entire chapter to public libraries in *Better Together: Restoring the American*

---

[13] Benedict Anderson, *Imagined Communities: Reflections on the Origin and Spread of Nationalism*, Revised Edition (London: Verso Books, 2006): 6.
[14] Edwards and Edwards, "Culture and the New Iraq," 331.

*Community*, calling them the Heartbeat of the Community.[15] Though Putnam uses several models as examples, only public libraries and churches are mentioned as formal, collective institutions capable of restoring community, and only libraries are welcoming to believers and nonbelievers alike. It is fascinating to see how Putnam, a non-librarian, conceptualizes the library, and likewise illuminating to see what he chooses to emphasize: "Death-of-the-library scenarios define libraries as information repositories. If they are no more than that, then their eventual displacement by more convenient electronic repositories would make persuasive sense. But the library is a gathering place, too, like an old town square or the corner grocer . . . people may go to the library looking mainly for information, but they find each other there."[16]

Putnam does two extraordinary things in these sentences. First, he immediately sees and understands libraries as something more than bookshelves and computer banks. He acknowledges the role of the library as information provider but asserts, as I do, that this is not all that the library does – that the library is "more than that." More importantly, though, he uses that last sentence to explain just why libraries are so much more than information repositories. While it may strike some readers as romantic rhetoric, his emphasis on the importance of finding community at the library cannot be overstated. The statement stands out because it points to the role of the library in *community* life – not just in *individual* life. How easily he could have written "people may go to the library looking mainly for information, but they find *themselves* there." How much more in keeping with the principles of our profession to focus on the impact that the library makes on the individual user. Instead, Putnam chooses to focus on the larger role of the library as a center of the community. Libraries "mirror their communities, showing residents who they are *collectively*" (emphasis added).[17] Recognizing that, as I noted, neither individuals nor libraries exist in vacuums, Putnam's chapter firmly places the role that the library plays in the *community*

---

[15] Putnam, *Better Together*, 34.
[16] Ibid., 49.
[17] Ibid., 51.

above both its role as information repository and point of service for the individual. While the individual may go to the library to find personally relevant information, he will also find there (in addition to what he seeks) an understanding that he is part of a larger organism, a group of individuals who collectively form his city or town and with whom he can create or restore a sense of community. The whole, for Putnam, most certainly becomes greater than the sum of its parts. In declaring the library not the *heart* of the community but the heart*beat* of the community, Putnam implies action, not just location. His powerful metaphor makes the library – the humble branch library, no less – the central, most essential, most active agent in the societal organism, pumping lifeblood throughout the community.

Of course, some of the strongest advocates for the role of libraries in community life come from within the profession. Like Putnam, David Carr sees the role of libraries in communities as extending beyond information to encompass the entirety of the community, noting that "processes, experiences, implications, differences . . . are always more important than the objects or the information we may find" in a library, while Nancy Kalikow Maxwell states that "people are drawn to libraries for reasons far more profound than simply needing information."[18] Carr envisions the community as "a kind of collaborative, perpetually unfinished mind, always in search of dialogue not only about its future, and the meaning of its past, but also about the paths that each of us has made" and writes that in considering this dialogue we must begin by "placing traditions of individualism aside" and recognizing that the dialogue is "the community's way to pay attention to its continuous themes, its folkways, and its memories. We pay attention in order to show . . . how deeply an interest in the life of the community is shared by all."[19] Here Carr begins moving us towards a broader understanding of community and the library's role within

---

[18] Carr, *A Place not a Place*, 126; Nancy Kalikow Maxwell, *Sacred Stacks: The Higher Purpose of Libraries and Librarianship* (Chicago: ALA Editions, 2006), 50.
[19] David Carr, *The Promise of Cultural Institutions*, American Association for State and Local History Book Series (Oxford: AltaMira Press, 2003), 63.

it. In this model, the library does not serve merely to provide information to a user, or even to document the past and help prepare for the future. Here, the library is the entity that draws the narratives of all the members of the community together. In allowing space for the dialogue about the paths individuals have made, the library becomes the institution that enables the disparate and unique members of a community to see themselves as united not in spite of the differences among them but perhaps because of them. Carr writes, "in every library, we see alternative cultures based on different assumptions than our own, we see the traces of individuals whose thinking is different and creative, and still a part of their time and our own."[20] We need to understand that this extends *beyond* the collections to encompass individuals and groups themselves. The richness of all of these different paths converging in the library is that individuals can come to appreciate that there are not only people in their community with shared experiences and interests but also people in their community whose life paths, in their very difference, ultimately enrich the community in new and unexpected, if not always comfortable, ways.

If we are to consider the works of Putnam, Carr and Maxwell and accept that the role that the library can and should play in community life extends beyond that of information provider, we must necessarily examine this relationship between libraries and communities in a deeper way. If libraries are to "reclaim their role as centers of the community" we have to begin to truly make an effort to conceptualize libraries as more than information, more than grand old buildings, and more even than places where people can find each other.[21] We need to look at libraries as representative of and symbolic of the communities in which they are located. To do so necessitates that we look not only at how libraries and their communities interact but also at how they intersect and inform each other and how, as symbolic of their communities, libraries thus become the nexus between our traditional understanding of ourselves and our roles and McCook's new model of librarianship.

20 Carr, *A Place not a Place*, xiii.
21 Maxwell, *Sacred Stacks*, 131.

Carr writes in *The Promise of Cultural Institutions* that "[i]t is the institution that is not just *for*, but *with* its community in trust, that thrives most fully."[22] I would take this a step further and argue that we should view the institution as not just *with* its community, but *of* its community. Conceptualizing the library in this way forces us to consider how our institutions both reflect and shape the culture of the community, and positions them as living, dynamic cultural organisms, not mere information repositories. Far from rejecting the role of the library as information provider, however, the scholarship on the cultural symbolism of libraries in community life actually invokes the importance of materials to *raise* the library beyond mere collections to explore the ways in which the material in question becomes not only representative of the community, but a living part of the community. Scholars like Knuth and Thomas Augst don't divorce the library from its materials.[23] Rather, they advocate for a deeper, more nuanced view of materials and collections, seeing in the information *symbolic power*. Collections thus become not simply utilitarian resources but vital components to the ways in which a community imagines itself. Augst succinctly states the problem of balancing the theoretical and philosophical aims of the library as a culturally situated institution with the more prosaic business of actually running a library: "the library has borne the particular weight of defining culture and devising means for its practical administration, all within a tangible set of problems regarding circulation, cataloging, and storage."[24] The problem, as I see it, is that librarians – with short staffs, small budgets, and the perceived threat of the Internet – become so busy with the administration of the library and so involved with the never-ending "tangible" problems that they don't consider the ways in which their institutions really are symbolic of the communities in which they serve. The focus we put on materials and processes in our profession is evidence of the enormous task of keeping our libraries op-

---

[22] Carr, *The Promise of Cultural Institutions*, 40.

[23] Knuth, *Libricide*; Thomas Augst, *Libraries as Agencies of Culture*, Series in Print Culture History in Modern America (Madison: University of Wisconsin Press, 2003).

[24] Augst, *Libraries as Agencies of Culture*, 6.

erational and of our continuous struggle to remain relevant. However, it is not by the materials and services alone that we will remain relevant. I would argue that these are not even the primary ways in which we will remain relevant. Rather, I encourage librarians to fight the tendency to privilege and prioritize materials and collections and start considering the ways in which those very materials and collections – and the library itself, of course – become symbolic of the community. That is, while it is wonderful to proclaim the library as the "hub of the community" it is essential to understand the library as *the* community itself and to use that as both the conceptual and actual basis of all services, decisions, and plans.[25]

I choose to think of libraries not only as cultural institutions (a model that to some degree favors the contents of the library as objects) but as culturally situated institutions. This model puts the focus on the life of the community and the role of the library within it. A culturally situated library is one that not only serves as the heart or heartbeat of the community, but one that represents, reflects, and shapes the community as a whole. The library becomes thus "culturally defined by" the community while at the same time "culturally defin[ing] the community that it serves."[26] In this symbiotic relationship materials become more than objects by which information is transmitted, and the library becomes the symbol of the life of the community.

Augst positions libraries as culturally symbolic because "what a library is depends on what it does: it is a social enterprise, a physical infrastructure, a symbolic site of collective memory."[27] Again refusing to divorce the library from its collections, Augst nonetheless emphasizes the role of the library in the creation of collective memory, stating that "[a]s a symbolic space, a type of collection, a kind of building, the library gives institutional form to our collec-

---

[25] Wayne Senville, "Libraries at the Heart of Our Communities," http://www.plannersweb.com/wfiles/w412.html (accessed 12 October 2009).
[26] Edwards and Edwards, "Libraries, Cultural Life, and Community Identity," 76.
[27] Augst, *Libraries as Agencies of Culture*, 6.

tive memory."[28] All that a library is and does positions it then as representative of the collective memory of the community. The library, in this model, is indeed more than an information repository, and the most important thing that the library does is help people understand themselves as a collective community with a shared past. This shared past becomes of significant importance in the potential for the community to survive as a group and plot its own future. I should note here that in no way do I minimize the potential conflicts that can arise when a community is not homogenous. I do suggest, however, that shared experiences shape communities as they form and evolve, even though those experiences may be understood in a variety of ways. Likewise, minority groups, immigrants, and communities-within-communities all have their own pasts that are unique and may historically be in conflict with the past of the larger community. However, I maintain that the library, particularly the public library, can serve as the one institution that can successfully broker what may seem like conflicting interests. I will discuss this in more detail as I move into an analysis of libraries and the principles of Article 27 later in the chapter.

Some of the most important work on libraries as symbols of cultural communities comes from Knuth. A scholar of cultural genocide, Knuth focuses on the negative impact that the destruction of libraries has had on communities across the globe. In *Libricide* she explores in depth the destruction of libraries in Nazi Germany, Greater Serbia, Kuwait, China and Tibet. The libraries she studies range from the National and University Library of Sarajevo, to academic, school and public libraries in China, to the personal library collections of scholars, theologians, and intellectuals. This broad range of libraries, and the wrenching accounts of the effects of their destruction on communities and individuals, serves as powerful evidence against the notion that only national libraries, museums, and archives are of significance to a culture. Recounting the burning by students of a middle school library in Shanghai, Kunth writes that "[i]t was their teachers . . . who grieved when books were burned. The distinguished professor You Xiaoli, who

---

28 Ibid., 24.

was physically tortured and then assigned to clean campus latrines for years, said later that the burning of books was worse than the physical and emotional abuse."[29] Can there be a more powerful example of why we must see the destruction of any library as a crime against culture? Is there any more powerful statement about the importance that all libraries play in the minds of a community? Libraries signify community identity as reflected through material culture.[30] This is no less true for school and public libraries than it is for national libraries and archives. And it is not only the information that is inextricably linked to the community. While the books in a public library may not be rare or unique or historically significant, the library itself – national library or middle school library or public library – serves to symbolize the higher aspirations and intellectual life of the community.

Knuth's seemingly simple observation that "[t]he contents of books and libraries reflect the social and cultural needs of their societies" is true for all libraries and, when one connects this assertion with Augst's reading of libraries as keepers of cultural memory, Putnam's claim that people find each other in the library and Carr's belief that the library supports dialogue, it becomes more clear that all books, all libraries, reflect their communities.[31] The symbolism of the library itself has a profound impact on the psyche of the community. Indeed, "the idea of the library is . . . significant and, in cases of cultural genocide, holds tremendous symbolic power. Such institutions, beyond even their collections, represent societies by the very fact of their existence. They function as important landmarks in the cultural geography of a people, and even if their collections are not irreplaceable, their destruction nonetheless serves as a moral blow to a community."[32]

Knuth has been tremendously influential in bringing to light libricide and its role in both cultural and actual genocide. The destruction of libraries, archives, museums and other cultural institu-

---

[29] Knuth, *Libricide*, 186.
[30] Ibid., 4.
[31] Ibid., 26.
[32] Edwards and Edwards, "Libraries, Cultural Life, and Community Identity," 79.

tions is no longer being seen as unfortunate collateral damage. The growing awareness that libraries do, in fact, serve as culturally situated institutions symbolic of the communities that claim them means that the global community turns a more critical and damning eye on the destruction of these institutions, reading the targeting of libraries as a deliberate act of war and an attempt at cultural obliteration. As I have noted in previous work, the testimony of Andras Riedlmayer before the International Criminal Tribunal of the former Yugoslavia helped make the destruction of libraries and other cultural institutions a prosecutable war crime and a crime against humanity – marking the first such instance of the conviction of individuals for the destruction of cultural property.[33] The change in international law, hugely significant (if not well known or easily enforceable in most cases) for both human rights and librarianship, provides concrete proof of the fact that libraries are indeed symbolic of the cultural life of the communities in which they serve. However, our growing understanding of libricide and the subsequent international attempts to prosecute individuals for this crime nonetheless represents a sort of negative emphasis on the importance of libraries in the cultural life of the community. That is, we tend to focus on libraries as symbolic of the community only when the library, and thus the community, is in danger.

What if we were to begin thinking of libraries as symbolic of their communities *before* instances of libricide (or any of the other, lesser, instances of controversy that tend usually to thrust the library into the front of people's minds)? Instead of retroactively claiming the library as culturally symbolic, what if we were to own this fact from the start and use it to inform all of our decisions, planning processes and services? Embracing our institutions as symbolic of the community in this way is not quite the same as the attempts of authors like Putnam to establish the library as central

---

[33] Ibid., 72; See also, Andras Riedlmayer, "Crimes of War, Crimes of Peace: Destruction of Libraries during and after the Balkan Wars of the 1990s," *Library Trends* 56:1 (Summer 2007): 107-132; and Andras Riedlmayer, *Destruction of Cultural Heritage in Bosnia-Herzegovina, 1992-1996: A Post-war Survey of Selected Municipalities* (Cambridge, MA: by the author, 2002).

to community life – the heartbeat of the community. While Putman and others rightly argue for the role of the library in community life, they do not explicitly claim the library as either symbolic of the community or the cultural life of that community. Rather, I suggest using Knuth's reading of the intersection of libraries and cultural identity and flipping it on its head. That is, instead of looking at the symbolic value of libraries as it is revealed through libricide, I suggest a positive reading of the symbolic value of libraries in the cultural life of the community. Through this lens we can then view the library as culturally situated and thus culturally symbolic in a proactive rather than reactive way. This shift in philosophy is not merely a rhetorical sleight of hand; to positively view libraries as symbolic in this manner will, I hope, provide librarians (and our patrons) a new way of envisioning our services, our missions and our role in local (and global) communities. Specifically, understanding and proactively claiming libraries as culturally symbolic is the best way for librarians to enter more fully into the human rights discourse and advocate for McCook's new model of librarianship. Without setting aside the human rights framework with which we have been working for years (the protection of individual rights) we must now look towards Article 27 and the ways in which libraries can use the language of human rights to add a new dimension to our understanding of our role in our communities and the cultures that comprise them. In short, it is time to move our understanding of libraries and community more deeply into the realm of human rights.

**Libraries and Article 27: Towards a New Vision of Librarianship**

Recently Samek and McCook and Phenix, long advocates for human rights in librarianship, have written more forcefully about the need to better integrate librarianship and human rights. In their recent work these authors have drawn on specific UDHR articles that have been or can be used to inform the practice of librarianship and the conceptualization of library work as human rights work. McCook and Phenix focus on how libraries and librarians have historically "internalized" and acted upon the principles of Article 7 (the right to equality before the law and equal protection against discrimination), Article 12 (the right to freedom from arbitrary interference in matters of privacy, family, home, or correspondence), and Article 19 (the right to freedom of opinion and expression and the right to hold opinions and seek, receive, and impart information and ideas) in their work.[34] In a conference paper Samek and Kevin Rioux highlight a list of articles and the rights therein that the International Center for Information Ethics (ICIE) asserts form the "basis for ethical thinking on the human rights responsibilities of library and information workers" and which include:

- Respect for the dignity of human beings (Article 1)
- Confidentiality (Articles 1, 2, 3, 6)
- Equality of opportunity (Articles 2 and 7)
- Privacy (Articles 3 and 12)
- Right to be protected from torture or cruel, inhuman, or degrading treatment or punishment (Article 5)
- Right to own property (Article 17)
- Right to freedom of thought, conscience and religion (Article 18)
- Right to freedom of opinion and expression (Article 19)
- Right to peaceful assembly and association (Article 20)
- Right to economic, social and cultural rights indispensable for dignity and the free development of personality (Article 22)
- Right to education (Article 26)
- Right to participate in the cultural life of the community (Article 27)
- Right to the protection of the moral and material interests concerning any scientific, literary, or artistic production (Article 27)[35]

---

[34] de la Peña McCook and Phenix, "Human Rights, Democracy and Librarians."

[35] Samek and Rioux, "Apologies, Boycotts, and Law Reform," 84-85. See also the International Center for Information Ethics, http://icie.zkm.de/

As we end the first decade of the twenty-first century we can see that McCook's vision of human rights as the new model for librarianship is becoming more explicit in the literature. These authors, educators and activists are not only bringing documents like the UDHR into the professional discourse, they are also pushing the profession, as I am, to look beyond Article 19 to other ways of bringing human rights principles to bear on librarianship. Both sets of authors point to the ways in which librarians actively *do* promote and protect human rights beyond Article 19, even though many librarians do not think of what they do on a day-to-day basis in those terms.[36] Samek and Rioux, while highlighting the ways in which librarians "walk the talk," significantly up the ante by citing the ICIE, an organization that firmly asserts that librarians have "responsibilities" – not just professional statements or tasks – centered around human rights. How these responsibilities take shape is open to interpretation, and Samek and Rioux, as well as McCook and Phenix, provide examples of what this model of librarianship has looked like in the past and what it might look like in the future. More important, though, is the assertion that a focus on human rights is indeed a professional responsibility – and one not so far removed from our standard understanding of our traditional duties. Such an assertion marks an important conceptual shift in the profession – one that must be capitalized upon and brought to bear on all aspects of librarianship. As I have mentioned, librarians have always been champions of certain human rights, even if they have not always used the language of human rights to describe their policies and actions. At the same time, though, the new writing on librarianship and human rights calls for both the claiming of library work as human rights work and the movement deeper into the UDHR as a means of forming a strong foundation from which to build upon the successes we've had in protecting individual rights.

One of the best ways to move beyond Article 19 is, as I have stated, through a professional focus on Article 27. This article, one

---

[36] For more discussion on librarians not claiming their work as human rights work see de la Peña McCook and Phenix, "Human Rights and Librarians," and Edwards and Edwards, "Libraries, Cultural Life, and Community Identity."

of six in the UDHR that deals with what have come to be called
cultural rights, provides the link between libraries, community, cultural life, and human rights and presents us with an opportunity to
proactively imagine the role that libraries can play in the promotion
and protection of the cultural life of a community. The first paragraph of the Article, and the paragraph on which I will focus in this
chapter, states in part that "everyone has the right to participate in
the cultural life of the community" – phrasing that, though certainly not unproblematic, has the potential of being realized
through libraries.

Article 27 in particular amongst the cultural rights articles has
come under fire for its wording, which can appear at once both
imperialistic and vague. The primary criticism levied against the
wording is that it suggests *one* cultural life in *one* community – a set
of conditions not found in the world in 1948 and certainly even
less so now.[37] This then raises the question, *whose* cultural life in
*which* community? Globalization has changed the ways in which we
understand the concepts of both community and culture and the
early 1950s saw UNESCO already struggling with the language of
the Article as well as with the concept of what constitutes "the cultural life of the community" and how that cultural life can be realized in actuality.

In 1952 UNESCO commissioned the "Programme of
UNESCO for 1952: Resolution 4.52: Study of the 'Right to Participate in Cultural Life' Basic Document."[38] UNESCO ordered the
study out of a desire to "analyse the philosophical and legal contents and the principal means of practical application of man's right
'freely to participate in the cultural life of the community.'"[39] Al-

---

[37] For more discussion about the role of the definite article in Article 27,
see Johannes Morsink, *The Universal Declaration of Human Rights: Origins,
Drafting and Intent* (Philadelphia: University of Pennsylvania Press, 2000);
and Morsink, "Cultural Genocide, The Universal Declaration, and Minority Rights," Human Rights Quarterly 24:1 (1999): 1009-1060.
[38] United Nations Educational, Scientific, and Cultural Organization
(UNESCO), *Study of the "Right to Participate in Cultural Life: Basic Document*,
Programme of UNESCO for 1952, Resolution 4.52.
[39] UNESCO, *Study of the "Right to Participate in Cultural Life*, 3.

ready the United Nations, the body that drafted the UDHR only four years earlier, was struggling with a two-pronged problem – the philosophical and legal content of Article 27 and the amorphous nature of cultural life. In some ways UNESCO was struggling with what I am considering here over 60 years later – how does one philosophically conceptualize and proactively apply Article 27? Indeed, all these years later the question is more complex due to factors such as globalization and the increased diversity to be found within even the smallest community.

UNESCO was well aware of the problems with Article 27 and was obviously concerned that the language in the Article could be read as vague or weak (though at this early stage the drafters of the study were less concerned with notions of imperialism, as we will see). In the opening paragraph on the "Implications of Article 27" the authors assert that "when it approved this text, the General Assembly of the United Nations was not merely adding a final touch to the Universal Declaration of Human Rights; it was stating, for the whole world, an entirely new principle, whose application may have tremendous repercussions."[40] The tone of this claim suggests that, four years after the drafting and approval of the UDHR, many already saw Article 27 as representing lesser rights. Anxious to reassure the world that Article 27 was not a rhetorical flourish, the authors of the study go to great lengths to highlight the importance of the cultural life of the community and the right to participate in it. They do acknowledge, however, that unlike other rights, articulating precisely what this Article means and how it is to be applied proved to be quite difficult, though no less essential:

> Unlike other rights, such as the right to work or the right to education, the practical implications of the right to participate in cultural life, and the measures necessary to make its proclamation effective, have not yet been clearly defined. Moreover, since it has to do with the highest of human aspirations, and since man, as a physical being, can survive without exercising it, it seems likely that the extent to which this right is applied may vary

---

[40] UNESCO, *Study of the "Right to Participate in Cultural Life,"* 4.

greatly according to the social and cultural conditions prevailing in different societies.[41]

Here we get a sense of from where the accusations of imperialism that have dogged Article 27 since its inception came. In the first section of the study the authors declare that "the context of Article 27. . . makes it clear that the term 'cultural life' is to be taken in the sense of 'intellectual life,'" although they acknowledge that "it should not. . .be overlooked that intellectual life is. . .bound up in the whole body of beliefs and customs proper to each group – what sociologists often mean by the term 'culture' in a wider sense."[42] The authors are clearly favoring "Culture" here – that thing which is not essential for survival and which they feel will "vary greatly" among societies. However, I would argue that "culture" should be read more broadly and that survival as a human in a society without culture is an impossibility, since it is impossible to function in a society without a "way of life." This tension between "Culture" and "culture" has plagued Article 27 for over 60 years and has remained a source of conflict. However, as I will show later, I believe that it is possible to reconcile this conflict to a great degree through the work of libraries in communities.

Overall, the study grapples with the problems of making sure that the rights inherent in Article 27 are accessible by all. The authors ask a series of questions about and intently ponder the definitions of culture, community, participation, and freedom. The effect, overall, is of one big, fascinating, philosophical and intellectual exercise. The study asks more questions than it answers, by far. This is, though, less frustrating than one might think, as the very act of asking the questions – and committing them to paper – provides an extraordinary glimpse into the ways in which Article 27 has been debated since its inception. Likewise, the act of commissioning the study shows that UNESCO took cultural rights seriously and was sincere in seeking modes of application that would allow for the free participation in cultural life.

---

[41] Ibid., 5.
[42] Ibid., 8.

Aside from being a fascinating glimpse into the struggles UNESCO encountered in applying Article 27, the study is extraordinary for my purposes because the authors identify early on the role that public institutions will play in the "preservation" and "promotion" of cultural life.[43] Section 2, "Forms of Participation," Part IV identifies, along with universities, schools, churches, museums, learned societies and a host of other institutions, libraries as one of the "bodies active in ensuring that all participate in cultural life."[44] In the last section of the study, on the practical implementation of Article 27, the authors list libraries first among those institutions that will preserve and promote cultural life:

> A special effort has been made to develop public libraries, which are of exceptional importance, not only to advanced societies, but also in regions which have engaged in literacy campaigns. These library projects are complimentary to fundamental and adult education programmes.

> A similar attempt has been made to develop and modernize museums so that, like public libraries, they may become active centres in the cultural life of peoples.[45]

Thus, as early as 1952, the United Nations recognized libraries as institutions absolutely instrumental for the successful application of Article 27, although again there is a clear sense of imperialism here that cannot be overlooked or excused. The study should, of course, be read in its historical context. However imperfect the application might be, though, UNESCO, in singling out libraries in this way, was seeking (as I am) a proactive approach for the promotion of the right freely to participate in the cultural life of the community and is concerned with how libraries can play a central role in such promotion. This study, which was seemingly overlooked by the profession, could prove to be an important document in establishing a new way of looking at the role libraries can play in the cultural life of the community and in developing a broader sense of the responsibility we have towards the promotion and protection of

---

43 Ibid., 7.
44 Ibid., 13.
45 Ibid., 20.

rights beyond those outlined in Article 19. We should reject the cultural imperialism suggested in the UNESCO study in favor of our current understandings of multicultural, responsive, and responsible library services (which are detailed in the excellent chapters later in this book) while also accepting that the connection between human rights and libraries is an important one.

UNESCO's study explicitly mentions libraries four times. However, the document is peppered with language that will be familiar to any librarian. In its philosophical musings, the study ponders the various ways in which individuals can participate in cultural life, the barriers to such participation, and the ways in which cultural life can be developed. The authors note, for example, that participation in cultural life does not have to be realized only through the actual production of art and culture on the part of an individual. "There may be a personal or non-creative contribution," they assert "in 'receptive' participation in cultural and scientific life," noting that such contribution may take "the form of study and reflection."[46] The authors note that "the conditions in which certain sections of the population work, and the conditions in which certain social groups live, form, as has often been pointed out, a major obstacle to their real freedom to take part in cultural life."[47] They continue on to state that "so far as certain sections of the population are concerned, freedom to participate in cultural life is restricted by psychological attitudes due to the consciousness of social inferiority, to education, or to the nature of cultural life itself, which may appear to the individual to have no reference to his own concerns" and conclude that "methods used to remove such obstacles" should "reference. . .the work of associations for the promotion of popular culture."[48]

The authors also note in a discussion on the "means of communication which can be used for the development of cultural life" that "'means of communication' is to be taken in a very wide sense, covering religious ceremonies, dramatic performances, concerts,

---

[46] Ibid., 11.
[47] Ibid., 16.
[48] Ibid., 17.

dancing and ballet, books, reviews, newspapers, public lectures, talks, broadcasting and television, film shows, permanent and temporary exhibitions, club meetings, discussion groups, organized visits to monuments or museums, etc."[49] Though the authors of the study clearly associate libraries strictly with books, public librarians in the United States will recognize here many, if not most, of the services their institutions offer patrons. In fact, UNESCO's description of the means of communication reads like a veritable laundry list of services provided by public libraries. With the possible exception of religious ceremonies, libraries – and public libraries in particular – are the one institution offering *all* of the means of communication, and more, listed as necessary for the development of cultural life.

If the UDHR will be essential in the establishment of human rights as the new model of librarianship, this half-century old UNESCO study will be foundational for understanding the ways in which libraries, particularly public libraries in the United States, must consider their role in promoting the cultural life of the community. Laid out here, in a document prepared by non-librarians for an international organization, we see reflected many of our own deepest beliefs and most inspiring services and actions. If there are doubts that libraries should take responsibility for making sure that the rights documented in Article 27 are upheld by our institutions this study should lay them to rest. People outside the profession made the explicit connection between libraries and cultural rights decades ago. Now, we should adopt this study as our own – highlighting the ways in which libraries, more than any other institution, have met the philosophical and actual challenges laid out by UNESCO, and pondering the ways in which we can continue to promote cultural rights through our services. We should proactively use the UNESCO study to help us take our first steps in moving beyond Article 19, for my position is clear – not only do libraries symbolize the communities in which they are claimed, they also symbolize, fully, in a way that no other institution can, the principles set forth in Article 27.

---

[49] Ibid., 12.

Despite the enormous value in the UNESCO study, however, it does have its shortcomings, as does Article 27 itself. The focus on traditional library services represented by books can be excused as an artifact of the times. The study does mention many of the services that our present libraries provide to the public, but it doesn't connect these services explicitly to libraries. What cannot be excused or overlooked, though, is the sense of imperialism that leads to the narrow focus on "Culture" or the notion that "Culture" serves only to better the individual or certain social groups. While this may be attributed to the historical context of the document, it is important that we look at culture in its most broad sense, as a way of life, and also take into account minority cultures and folkways in addition to high culture or popular culture (which often favors mainstream society in its representations). While the study gives short shrift to these other aspects of culture, they are becoming increasingly important and indeed valued in our globalized and heterogeneous world. The diversity of cultures is shaping our communities and, as an institution *of* the community, the library is the natural nexus of this diversity and the best place to incorporate seemingly conflicting aspects of culture.

If libraries are to truly be symbolic of their communities, and of Article 27 in its best sense, they must incorporate all aspects of culture. Fortunately, this is something that librarians, particularly in public libraries, have been doing for years. Librarians have been concerned with serving the various cultures that make up their communities and have consciously made efforts to provide services for minority populations, new immigrants, and other communities-within-community, even while maintaining a commitment to and providing access to what is traditionally considered high culture. Have librarians considered this human rights work? Probably not. Have they used Article 27 as the driving factor in creating these services? No. This, of course, does not mean that the services have not been meeting the needs of the community. However, in thinking about this work as human rights work and in framing it in the language of Article 27 we can begin to get a sense of new ways in which we can advocate for our institutions and our communities. That is, we can begin to take a proactive stance on the importance of our institutions in the cultural life of our communities – even if, or perhaps especially because, that cultural life can often look like a patchwork quilt. As the nexus of "Culture" and "culture," and as symbols of community and Article 27, libraries are uniquely positioned to truly reflect, promote, and shape the cultural life of the community. The first two actions, as I have stated, are something that libraries have done for decades. The third, however, is something that libraries rarely claim they do, perhaps because our professional commitment to neutrality makes us wary of actively trying to influence our patrons or communities. I propose, however, that shaping the culture of the community in which a library is situated is an essential part of ensuring that the rights set forth in Article 27 are met for all members of a community and that human rights prosper in general.

I wrote earlier in this chapter that we must see libraries as more than static repositories of material, that they must do more than simply provide access to information. It is essential that we see libraries as active, dynamic agents of culture that reflect and promote the community and, in doing so, become places of meaning that stretch beyond information to encompass the very fabric of the cultural life of the community. The first way that libraries can do this is by accurately reflecting the cultural life of the communities in which they are situated. This means, contrary to the notion of "Culture" put forth in the UNESCO study and in some readings of Article 27, that libraries work to represent as fully as possible all the cultures they serve. This has traditionally been done through a focus on staffing, collections and programming. Usually libraries routinely employ at least one of these strategies, if not some combination of all three, to meet the needs of the diversity of cultures in the community. For example, libraries will actively recruit and hire multilingual librarians as part of their efforts to serve members of a community. Indeed, the recruitment of librarians with diverse backgrounds, including the ability to speak languages other than English, is an extremely important way of making sure that everyone has the right to participate in the cultural life of a community, since language is fundamental to culture and since the presence of people in the library who can communicate in the preferred cultural milieu creates a welcoming environment and sends a message about the importance to the library of that community. Library schools, with support from ALA, also seek to recruit and retain diverse students so that these graduates can then best serve a variety of communities across the United States.[50]

When it is not possible to reflect the cultural life of the community through the hiring of staff, libraries will often build collections of materials that meet the needs of the community – for example, foreign language materials, or LGBTIQ materials, or materials about local history. These are all very traditional ways of reflecting the cultural life of the community, and they all point to the needs and interests of segments of society that we typically consider when talking about diversity. Collection development is one of the primary ways that libraries can reflect the cultural life of the community, and librarians traditionally have been very careful in making sure that at least some part of the collection serves all interests of the community. Could libraries do better? Yes – a shelf full of foreign language books may be a nice gesture, but it may not be meeting the full needs of the community. In this way, making Article 27 the bedrock of collection development encourages librarians to truly and deeply consider whether or not the materials in the library accurately reflect the community and meet its needs. It transforms collection development work into human rights work and in the best, most ideal, situations it helps ensure that the collection is not homogenized, thus partially mitigating the criticism that the destruction of a public library, for example, doesn't matter because all collections are roughly the same. In this way library materials do become so much more than objects because we consider them in light of what they do, not just what they are.

Of course, sometimes it is simply not possible to create a collection that meets the needs of the cultural life of everyone in the community. Fortunately, acquisitions and staffing are not the only ways in which a library can reflect the cultural life of the commu-

---

[50] See American Library Association, "Spectrum Scholarship Program," http://www.ala.org/ala/aboutala/offices/diversity/spectrum/index.cfm (accessed 28 March 2010).

nity. Library programming has been a very successful way of high-lighting the diversity of cultures in a community, and libraries have hosted story times, musical and dramatic performances, and culinary programs that feature the richness of various cultures. Evenings of music, traditional storytelling, and craft workshops are some of the many ways in which libraries can highlight the cultures that comprise the community, particularly when individuals or groups from the culture or community-within-a-community are involved, as they should be whenever possible. And all of this, staffing, collection building and programming, represents merely one facet of the library. The library that one night hosts an ethnic cooking class may the next night hold a language class and the next night hold a classical concert, followed by a landscape painting workshop, and rounding out the week with a book group that studies the classics of the Western Canon. One does not need to sacrifice "Culture" to meet the right of everyone to participate in the cultural life of the community. Indeed, the library serves as a very real example of the interaction between and blending of cultures and of the inherently dynamic nature of culture (keeping in mind that the role of the library should not be to force assimilation into mainstream society, though it has unfortunately and inexcusably been used to those ends in the past).

In addition to reflecting the cultural life of the community the library can also turn to Article 27 as a foundational guide for *promoting* the cultural life of the community. If libraries are truly to be of the community, their promotion of the various cultures that make up the community is essential. In addition to the diverse cultural programming mentioned above, and returning to an earlier example, cultural programming might also focus on areas of interest to many members of the community through lectures or workshops on gardening, or local history, for example. As with collection development, programming does not have to focus solely on minority groups or communities-within-community. However, ensuring that all of the cultures in a community are represented in some way does two interesting things – it confirms to these multiple communities that they are welcome and respected, and that their languages and customs are valuable additions to the community as a whole.

Likewise, it helps members of the community who may identify as more mainstream, or as members of a different community-within-community, realize that the community as a whole is a rich and complicated organism that can be encountered and better understood at the library. It stretches the idea of community to one that is broad and rich and encompasses all aspects of what actually makes up the community.

The library, in promoting the *cultures* of the community, can be the most powerful agent for helping the community understand its combined, shared *culture*. As I have noted, culture is not static, and the promotion by the library of all the cultures in a community – if done well – encourages the community to look at itself in a new way. In this way, the community with a rich past in colonial New England, for example, also is the community of nineteenth-century industry, and the community of Greek and Dominican immigrants, and home to a thriving Orthodox Jewish population. Are all of these, in their difference, mutually exclusive? They shouldn't be – and if the library promotes all of these cultures eventually all of the cultures act upon each other so that they together make up the character of a place and a people. Does this mean that the blending occurs to such an extent that the dominant cultural markers of one group eventually disappear? Ideally, this should not be the case, although there is danger of this that the library must recognize and resist. Even if the cultures do not act upon each other in an obvious way, I return to Putnam in recognizing that when one goes to the library and finds "others" there, one can begin getting a better sense of exactly what comprises his community. Though this is sometimes a fraught experience, and certainly one not without a whole variety of problems, I suggest that these disparate groups can imagine themselves as part of something larger, something that encompasses them all – not in spite of their differences but because of their shared experiences. Anderson notes that "all communities. . .are imagined."[51] It is through a library, through the promotion of all aspects of the cultural life of the community with an eye towards human rights work, that this can happen. I in no

---

[51] Anderson, *Imagined Communities*, 6.

way intend this to read as a utopian vision of what the library can do in a community – but I do believe, as I stated earlier, that all of the richness of this multiplicity of cultural life does contribute to a shared cultural life and to the imagining of the community as a whole.

Promotion of cultural rights does one more very important thing – it helps establish the library as a central part of the community, indeed as the symbol of the community. In promoting the *cultures* that comprise the *culture* of the community the library necessarily takes a more active role within the community, or at least it should. This is an area in which using Article 27 as a foundation for library services can prove most useful for conceptualizing the ways in which libraries will operate in the twenty-first century. Many libraries, as I mentioned, do all kinds of cultural programming and many times this type of programming does serve to make a segment of the population feel welcome while at the same time exposing other segments of the population to the richness in their own community. However, if libraries were to, from the start, use Article 27 as their *reason* for promoting such diversity through programming and other services they would necessarily have to become more active in advocating for the importance of such interactions from a human rights perspective. That is, if a library were to host a program not only because it would provide an evening of unique and interesting entertainment but because such programming would help the community better understand itself and encourage the participation of everyone in cultural life, the community would benefit tremendously and the individuals within the community would see the library as a leader in the promotion of cultural life, community interaction, and human rights. And while many libraries do plan programming to promote certain cultures or to educate their communities, the proactive application of Article 27 to all aspects of the planning and execution of such events would establish for the library a new place of ethical high ground and would help cement human rights as a guiding force in librarianship.

Finally, promotion of the various cultures that make up the whole of the cultural life of the community naturally leads to the opportunity for the library to actively *shape* the cultural life of the community. In bringing all the cultures together and in helping the community imagine that these parts create the whole of cultural life, the library would chart a new course for the community, one that welcomes and celebrates all present and historical aspects of the community and leaves room for the new interpretations of the community in the future. The library would become an active agent in the creation of culture in the community, not in such a way as to force the homogenization of the community or the assimilation of parts of the community, but in such a way as to highlight the richness of the cultures in a community and to reaffirm that all of the cultures together combine to create an extraordinary whole. In a sense the library would be a tonic to globalization which, while increasing the diversity of communities also manages to decrease the manifestations of culture through force or necessity or neglect. In embracing Article 27 as the basis for shaping the culture of a community public libraries would be shaken free from their position of studied neutrality and would become in a real, proactive, positive way symbolic of their communities – and would at the same time encourage their communities to recognize this fact as a fact in and of itself, not as something to reflect upon after a crisis. As institutions, libraries are perhaps the best answer to the problem that plagues Article 27 regarding *whose* culture in *which* community. It is in this interaction, this reflecting and promoting and shaping of cultures, that we come to understand that culture is not static, that "culture" does not have to be in conflict with "Culture," and that in fact *all* of these different cultures, and all of these different groups, are *exactly* what make up *the community*.

# Cultural Rights and Library Development and Discourse in Sub-Saharan Africa: Is the Colonial Legacy Still Alive?

Natalia Taylor Poppeliers

1. Everyone has the right freely to participate in the cultural life of the community, to enjoy the arts and to share in scientific advancement and its benefits.

2. Everyone has the right to the protection of the moral and material interests resulting from any scientific, literary or artistic production of which he is the author.

*Universal Declaration of Human Rights, Article 27*

## Introduction

Library development in Sub-Saharan Africa has historically been dominated by Western traditions and influenced by the former colonial countries and others in the global North.[1] During the second half of the twentieth century the literature on African librarianship often reflected a discomfort expressed by African librarians at the widening abyss between Western models of librarianship and local realities of Sub-Saharan communities, cultures, and resources. In contrast, the library literature from the global North was frequently marked by tones of paternalism and idealism with many discussions concluding that if Northern libraries, institutions, and associations

---

[1] Paul Sturges and Richard Neill, *The Quiet Struggle: Information and Libraries for the People of Africa*, 2nd ed. (London: Mansell, 1998), 88-114.

adopted African libraries and assisted in the flow of information and resources from North to South, the problem of information poverty and stunted library development could be alleviated.[2] The twenty-first century has witnessed the expansion of globalization, the development of new information and communication technologies (ICTs), a strengthened open access movement, the holding of the World Summit on the Information Society (WSIS), and the global financial crisis – all of which have impacted libraries and institutions around the world. This chapter examines how the discourse on library development in Sub-Saharan Africa has changed in the new millennium given the events and trends mentioned above. Additionally, I explore recent rhetoric on African library development and investigate the extent to which this new rhetoric recognizes or engages the cultural rights expressed in Article 27 of the Universal Declaration of Human Rights (UDHR). At the core of this discussion are the questions, "What are cultural rights?" and "Why should librarians and information workers be concerned with cultural rights?"

**Cultural Rights: A Brief Overview**

The UDHR was adopted by the General Assembly of the United Nations on December 10, 1948 and later codified into two covenants – the International Covenant on Civil and Political Rights (ICCPR) and the International Covenant on Economic, Social and Cultural Rights (ICESCR) – both of which are legally binding to those states that have ratified them. The UDHR, ICCPR, and ICESCR together constitute the International Bill of Human Rights and serve as the core basis for other conventions and protocols expanding on or clarifying these rights. Within the UDHR, Articles 22 through 27 address specific economic, social and cultural rights.[3]

---

[2] Peter Johan Lor and Johannes Britz, "Knowledge Production from an African Perspective: International Information Flows and Intellectual Property," *International Information and Library Review* 37 (2005): 61-76.
[3] Mashood A. Baderin and Robert McCorquodale, "The International Covenant on Economic, Social and Cultural Rights: Forty Years of Development," in *Economic, Social and Cultural Rights in Action*, ed. Mashood A.

Of the UDHR Articles, only Article 27 specifically addresses cultural rights although several scholars have argued that there are close links between cultural rights and other rights delineated in the International Bill of Human Rights.[4] Other scholars have discussed the "transversal character" of cultural rights, arguing that they cover economic, social, civil and political rights, and thus embody the indivisibility of all human rights.[5] In her elaboration on the transversal quality of cultural rights, Yvonne Donders summarizes it thus:

> In short, the broad concept of culture, including not only cultural products but also process-oriented aspects such as association, language, religion and education, implies that cultural rights include many different human rights, which may have a civil, cultural, economic, political or social origin. Cultural rights are not only the rights to create and enjoy cultural products: they include rights to have access to and participate in culture, as well as rights that concern the broad concept of culture, including freedoms of association, language and religion and the right to education. Finally, cultural rights refer to the cultural dimension of other human rights, such as the rights to health, housing and food. Cultural rights are consequently more than merely those rights that explicitly refer to culture, but include all human rights

---

Baderin and Robert McCorquodale (Oxford: Oxford University Press, 2007), 3-24.

[4] For a discussion of the connection between cultural rights and other rights such as the rights to education, freedom of expression and information, and religion, see Asbjørn Eide, "Cultural Rights as Individual Human Rights" in *Economic, Social and Cultural Rights: A Textbook*, 2nd. ed., ed. Asbjørn Eide, Catarina Krause, and Allan Rosas (Dordrecht: Martinus Nijhoff, 2001), 289-301.

[5] Patrice Meyer-Bisch, "Les Droits Culturels Forment-ils une Catégorie Spécifique de Droits de l'Homme? Quelques difficultés logiques," in *Les Droits Culturels: Une Catégorie Sous-Développée de Droits de l'Homme: VIIIe Colloque Interdisiplinaire sur les Droits de l'Homme à l'Université de Fribourg 28-30 Novembre 1991 Actes et Documents de Suivi*, ed. Patrice Meyer-Bisch (Fribourg, Switzerland : Editions Universitaires, 1993), 17-43.

that protect or promote components of the cultural identity of individuals and communities as part of their dignity.[6]

Similar to the sole explicit reference to culture in the UDHR, the only article specifically addressing cultural rights in the ICESCR is Article 15. Given the minimal mention of cultural rights in the UDHR and the ICESCR, it is easy to see why some authors have considered these rights the "failed Cinderella of the international human rights lexicon."[7] ICESCR Article 15 includes the core components mentioned in UDHR Article 27 of the rights to take part in cultural life, to enjoy the benefits of scientific progress and its applications, and to benefit from the protection of the moral and material interests resulting from any scientific, literary, or artistic production of which he is the author. In addition to these components, it includes the following specifications:

> 2. The steps to be taken by the States Parties to the present Covenant to achieve the full realization of this right shall include those necessary for the conservation, the development and the diffusion of science and culture.

> 3. The States Parties to the present Covenant undertake to respect the freedom indispensable for scientific research and creative activity.

> 4. The States Parties to the present Covenant recognize the benefits to be derived from the encouragement and development of international contacts and co-operation in the scientific and cultural fields. [8]

Dominic McGoldrick has argued that there is a significant difference between the "right to take part in cultural life" as stated in the

---

[6] Yvonne Donders, "The Legal Framework of the Right to Take Part in Cultural Life," in *Human Rights in Education, Science and Culture: Legal Developments and Challenges*, ed. Yvonne Donders and Vladimir Volodin (Aldershot, Hampshire, UK: Ashgate, 2007), 231-272.

[7] Yvonne M. Donders, *Towards a Right to Cultural Identity?* (Antwerpen: Intersentia, 2002), 65-68.

[8] United Nations, *International Covenant on Economic, Social, and Cultural Rights* (1966), Article 15, sec. 2-4, http://www.unhchr.ch/html/menu3/b/a_cescr.htm (accessed June 1, 2009).

ICESCR and the right "freely to participate in the cultural life of the community" as presented in the UDHR in that the right to participate "in *the* cultural life of *the* community" implies a singular cultural life of a singular community.[9] Despite this, the contemporary understanding of this right is that there can be many communities in a state, all of which have cultural rights. The *Reporting Guidelines of the Committee on ESC Rights* specify that individuals have the right to take part in the cultural life which he or she considers pertinent as well as the right to manifest his or her own culture.[10] I will explore these distinctions, and their potential meaning and implications for African libraries, further in this chapter.

There are several reasons why cultural rights remain marginalized within the larger human rights documentation.[11] There has tended to be a wide spectrum of interpretation for the term "cultural rights." On one side of the spectrum is the intellectual idea of culture and the processes of its creators as relevant only to the areas of art, literature, and music. On the other side of the spectrum is the anthropological sense of culture as a "way of life."[12] Additionally, the term "culture" has often been discussed in broad and vague terms, there has been a lack of consensus on which rights are cultural, and a lack of consensus on how best to implement them. Few states have been eager to adopt specific regulations in relation

---

[9] Dominic McGoldrick, "Culture, Cultures, and Cultural Rights," in *Economic, Social and Cultural Rights in Action* (see note 3), 447-473; for a discussion of the difference between the right "to" culture and the right to take part "in" cultural life see UN Committee on Economic, Social and Cultural Rights, Seventh Session 23 November-11 December 1992, *Implementation of the International Covenant on Economic, Social and Cultural Rights: Implementation of Cultural Rights: Analytical Study of Article 15 of the International Covenant on Economic, Social and Cultural Rights*, prepared by Samba Cor Konaté, E/C.12/1992/WP.4, 25 November 1992.

[10] McGoldrick, "Culture, Cultures, and Cultural Rights," 453.

[11] Donders, "The Legal Framework," 232.

[12] McGoldrick, "Culture, Cultures, and Cultural Rights," 499; see also Eide, "Cultural Rights as Individual Rights,"; see also Jane K. Cowan, "Introduction," in *Culture and Rights: Anthropological Perspectives*, ed. Jane K. Cowan, Marie-Bénédicte Dembour, and Richard A. Wilson (Cambridge: Cambridge University Press, 2001), 1-26.

to cultural rights, most states do not consider them to imply positive state obligations, and many states fear that strengthening cultural rights may lead to tension and instability within society because it may empower certain communities which will challenge
national unity.[13] Despite this marginalization and ambiguity, several
scholars have argued that the idea of culture in the international
human rights regime has evolved over the years from one narrowly
focused on the elitist concepts referring only to the fine arts and
literature to a much broader concept presenting culture as a process which includes components relating to, *inter alia,* language, religion and education.[14] UNESCO has been at the heart of the elaboration and delineation of additional standards related to collective
and individual cultural rights.[15]

An additional paradox when considering cultural rights is their
dual nature in that they encompass both individual and "group
rights" or the collective rights of peoples.[16] Most human rights, as
delineated in the International Bill of Human Rights, have an individualist perspective whereas cultural rights, by their nature, have a
strong group or communitarian aspect.[17] While legal provisions
may be defined as individual rights, the enjoyment of cultural rights
is firmly connected to communities.[18] Freedom of religion, expression, and association are viewed as individual rights although they
are essential to the development of culture. To these have been
added new claims from communities, such as the collective right to

---

[13] Donders, "The Legal Framework," 232.

[14] Ibid., 232.

[15] For an overview of this, see Janusz Symonides, "The History of the
Paradox of Cultural Rights and the State of the Discussion with
UNESCO" in *Les Droits Culturels* (see note 5), 47-72; for a discussion of
UNESCO's involvement in the relationship between the definition of the
term "culture" and the universalism versus relativism debate, see Thomas
Hylland Eriksen, "Between Universalism and Relativism: A Critique of
the UNESCO Concept of Culture" in *Culture and Rights* (see note 12), 127-
48.

[16] Donders, "The Legal Framework," 234.

[17] McGoldrick, "Culture, Cultures, and Cultural Rights," 450.

[18] Donders, "The Legal Framework," 234.

the development and protection of cultural identity, the right not to have an alien culture imposed on it, the rights of peoples to their own cultural heritage, and the right to participate in the cultural heritage of the world.[19] Related to this paradox, Thomas Hylland Eriksen has argued that the very use of the term culture is misleading and he has advocated that, rather than using the broad and "cozy blanket of culture," it would be better to identify and speak of specific rights such as freedom of religion, language, food habits, ritual practices, local political practices, and so on.[20]

Further discussions on cultural rights have pointed out that the rhetoric of cultural rights generally focuses on the rights of minorities or indigenous peoples with the assumption being that majority cultures can take care of themselves.[21] Related to this, Asbjørn Eide has written about the tension that exists between the individual as the producer of culture when that individual finds existing traditions unacceptable or insufficient:

> Existing cultural traditions may be considered repressive by some, legitimizing hierarchies, feudal or clan-like with rampant paternalism, inequality and lack of freedom; they may give almost a claustrophobic feeling. Some individuals therefore challenge existing patterns of culture, in favour of innovation and change. The right to innovate and to challenge is not only a significant part of individual cultural rights, but also a cause of tension.[22]

Thus, individual cultural rights can both coincide with collective human rights and represent a challenge to them as dominant elites within states or subregions seek to preserve their power based on

---

[19] Ibid., 234; see also Lyndel V. Prott, "Cultural Rights as Peoples' Rights in International Law," in *The Rights of Peoples*, ed. James Crawford (Oxford: Clarendon Press, 1988), 93-106; see also Meyer-Bisch "Les Droits Culturels," 18-19, 38-39.

[20] Eriksen, "Between Universalism and Relativism," 142.

[21] McGoldrick, "Culture, Cultures, and Cultural Rights," 451; see, for example, Donders, *Towards a Right*, Chapters VII, VIII and XI.

[22] Eide, "Cultural Rights as Individual," 291.

cultural traditions that are then challenged by individuals negatively affected by those traditions.[23]

As mentioned earlier, the idea that a state, group, or individual has a single culture has been strongly challenged. An alternative understanding has emerged signaling a state of multiple-cultures and individuals enveloped in an extensive system of sub-cultures.[24] McGoldrick, in his discussion of U.S. opposition to the *Convention on the Protection and Promotion of the Diversity of Cultural Expressions*,[25] points out that the concept of culture as a human right is a form of resistance to the commodification tendency that has come about through the economic liberalization and de-territorialization of markets that has spread with increased globalization. He argues that the U.S. ideology continues to envision "culture" as more individualistic and property-oriented rather than as "more communal, conservative, traditional, and linked to inheritance, and not necessarily being linked to an economic exchange of any sort."[26] These paradoxes, and the various and evolving notions of culture, represent a continuing challenge to universal human rights discourse at the macro or conceptual level.[27] Conflicts of property vs. communal and individual vs. collective often manifest in discussions of cultural rights and library development in Africa.

### Why Should Librarians be Concerned with Cultural Rights?

I will now explore two primary reasons why librarians must be concerned with cultural rights. Foremost, libraries are specifically mentioned in several international human rights documents regarding cultural rights. For example, the Committee on ESC Rights has issued detailed reporting guidelines concerning cultural rights.[28] In

---

[23.] Ibid., 300-301.

[24] McGoldrick, "Culture, Cultures, and Cultural Rights," 450.

[25] The Convention was adopted by the 33rd General Conference of UNESCO in October 2005 and entered into force on 18 March 2007.

[26] McGoldrick, "Culture, Cultures, and Cultural Rights," 470.

[27] Ibid., 449.

[28] UN Committee on Economic, Social and Cultural Rights, *Revised General Guidelines Regarding the Form and Contents of Reports to be Submitted by States*

this document the Committee specifically asks for States to report on the following in relation to Article 15 of the ICESCR:

a. Availability of funds for the promotion of cultural development and popular participation in cultural life, including public support for private initiative.

b. The institutional infrastructure established for the implementation of policies to promote popular participation in culture, such as cultural centres, museums, libraries, theatres, cinemas, and in traditional arts and crafts.

c. Promotion of cultural identity as a factor of mutual appreciation among individuals, groups, nations and regions.

d. Promotion of awareness and enjoyment of the cultural heritage of national ethnic groups and minorities and of indigenous peoples.

e. Role of mass media and communications media in promoting participation in cultural life.

f. Preservation and presentation of mankind's cultural heritage.

g. Legislation protecting the freedom of artistic creation and performance, including the freedom to disseminate the results of such activities, as well as an indication of any restrictions or limits imposed on the freedom.

h. Professional education in the field of culture and art.

i. Any other measures taken for the conservation, development and diffusion of culture.[29]

In addition to libraries being explicitly mentioned in part B, I would argue that libraries are implicated in parts C through G due to collection, access, and censorship practices and policies inherent in library and information work. Part C, concerning the "promotion of cultural identity as a factor of mutual appreciation," represents an opportunity for libraries and information workers to blend the right "to participate in the cultural life of the community" with

---

*Parties under Articles 16 and 17 of the International Covenant on Economic, Social and Cultural Rights*, E/C.12/1991/1, 17 June 1991.
[29] Ibid., 19-20.

the right "to take part in cultural life" by providing spaces and services where multiple community identities are supported and where
community members are encouraged to learn, appreciate, and share
aspects of significant divergent identities. The reporting guidelines
go on to elaborate reporting mechanisms for parts 2-4 of Article 15
related to the right of everyone to enjoy the benefits of scientific
progress and the right of everyone to benefit from the protection
of the moral and material interests resulting from any scientific,
literary or artistic work of which he or she is the author. These also
relate directly to library collections, access, and community relations.

    In addition to the reporting guidelines of the ICESCR, the
UNESCO *Universal Declaration on Cultural Diversity*[30] was later codified in the *Convention on the Protection and Promotion of the Diversity of
Cultural Expressions*[31] and was adopted by the General Conference
of UNESCO on October 20, 2005 and entered into force on
March 18, 2007. This document, while not explicitly mentioning
libraries, implicates in its preamble specific areas where libraries
continue to play a key role in cultural life. Relevant paragraphs include [emphases in original]:

> ...*Recognizing* the importance of traditional knowledge as a source
> of intangible and material wealth, and in particular the knowl-
> edge systems of indigenous peoples, and its positive contribution
> to sustainable development, as well as the need for its adequate
> protection and promotion,
>
> *Recognizing* the need to take measures to protect the diversity of
> cultural expressions, including their contents, especially in situa-
> tions where cultural expressions may be threatened by the possi-
> bility of extinction or serious impairment...

---

[30] The *Universal Declaration on Cultural Diversity* was adopted by the General
Conference of UNESCO on November 2, 2001.
[31] UNESCO, *Convention on the Protection and Promotion of the Diversity of Cultural Expressions*, CLT.2005/CONVENTION DIVERSITE-CULT REV.,
20 October 2005.

*Being aware* that cultural diversity is strengthened by the free flow of ideas, and that it is nurtured by constant exchanges and interaction between cultures,

*Reaffirming* that freedom of thought, expression and information, as well as diversity of the media, enable cultural expressions to flourish within societies,...

*Recalling* that linguistic diversity is a fundamental element of cultural diversity, and reaffirming the fundamental role that education plays in the protection and promotion of cultural expressions,

*Taking into account* the importance of the vitality of cultures, including for persons belonging to minorities and indigenous peoples, as manifested in their freedom to create, disseminate and distribute their traditional cultural expressions and to have access thereto, so as to benefit them for their own development...

*Recognizing* the importance of intellectual property rights in sustaining those involved in cultural creativity...

*Noting* that while the processes of globalization, which have been facilitated by the rapid development of information and communication technologies, afford unprecedented conditions for enhanced interaction between cultures, they also represent a challenge for cultural diversity, namely in view of risks of imbalances between rich and poor countries...[32]

These are but two examples of libraries being either explicitly or implicitly connected with human rights documentation.

The second reason why librarians and information workers should be concerned about cultural rights is that the core ideals of the library profession as developed in the Anglo-American tradition implicate cultural rights. While at first glance the *Library Bill of Rights* of the American Library Association (ALA)[33] appears to fo-

---

[32] Ibid., 1-2.
[33] American Library Association, "Library Bill of Rights,"
http://www.ala.org/ala/aboutala/offices/oif/statementspols/statementsi
f/librarybillrights.cfm (accessed May 31, 2009). The Library Bill of Rights was adopted by the American Library Association (ALA) Council in 1948 and amended in 1961, 1967, 1980, inclusion of "age" reaffirmed 1996. For

cus primarily on those individual rights set forth in Article 19 of the UDHR concerning access to information and expression, there are several instances where group and/or cultural rights are implicated [emphases added]:

> I. Books and other library resources should be provided for the interest, information, and enlightenment of all people *of the community* the library serves. Materials should not be excluded because of the *origin, background, or views* of those contributing to their creation...

> IV. Libraries should cooperate with all persons *and groups* concerned with resisting abridgment of free expression and free access to ideas.

> V. A person's right to use a library should not be denied or abridged because of *origin, age, background, or views.*

> VI. Libraries which make exhibit spaces and meeting rooms available to the public they serve should make such facilities available on an equitable basis, regardless of the beliefs or affiliations of individuals *or groups* requesting their use.[34]

It is imperative that if librarians and information workers in the U.S. are to adhere to this fundamental document of our profession, they must give careful attention to the area of cultural rights.

Obligations regarding cultural rights and libraries are also present in our international professional bodies. The International Federation of Library Associations (IFLA), the leading international body representing the library and information services profession, was founded in 1927 in Edinburgh, Scotland and now has approximately 1600 members in 150 countries.[35] In December 2004, the Governing Board of IFLA endorsed a model for IFLA's operations which has been labeled *IFLA's Three Pillars.* Of these

---

a full discussion of the original document approved in 1939 and the history of its revisions see Office for Intellectual Freedom of the ALA, "Library Bill of Rights: The Policy History," in *Intellectual Freedom Manual,* 7th ed., (Chicago: American Library Association, 2006), 57-72.

[34] ALA, "Library Bill of Rights."

[35] International Federation of Library Associations, "About IFLA," http://www.ifla.org/en/about (accessed May 26, 2009).

three pillars, the Society Pillar relates most specifically to cultural rights. The Society Pillar is defined thus:

> The Society Pillar focuses on the role and impact of libraries and information services in society and the contextual issues that condition and constrain the environment in which they operate across the world. Those issues are addressed currently through FAIFE, CLM, Blue Shield, and our advocacy in the World Summit on the Information Society (WSIS) and other arenas.[36]

The "contextual issues that condition and constrain" the way that libraries and information services operate across the world, while sometimes implicating individual political or civil rights, often directly involve cultural and group rights. While the Committee on Free Access to Information and Freedom of Expression (FAIFE) deals primarily with the former, the Blue Shield Network[37] and the WSIS have both addressed cultural and group rights.

Similarly, the IFLA Statutes, adopted at the IFLA Council meeting in Québec City, Canada on August 14, 2008 imply cultural rights in the following sections [emphases added]:

> 2.2 To achieve its purpose, the Federation seeks:

> 2.2.1 to promote high standards of delivery of library and information services and professional practice, *as well as the accessibility, protection, and preservation of documentary cultural heritage.* This is done through the enhancement of professional education, the development of professional standards, the dissemination of best practice and the advancement of relevant scientific and professional knowledge;...

> 2.3 In pursuing its purpose, the Federation shall seek to demonstrate the following core values:...

---

[36] Ibid., "IFLA's Three Pillars," http://www.ifla.org/en/three-pillars (accessed May 26, 2009).

[37] The Blue Shield Network defines itself as the cultural equivalent of the Red Cross – working for the protection of the world's cultural heritage by coordinating preparations to meet and respond to emergency situations. See Blue Shield Network, "About the Blue Shield," http://www.ancbs.org/index.php?option=com_content&view=article&id=41&Itemid=19 (accessed May 31, 2009).

2.3.2 the belief that people, *communities* and organizations need
universal and equitable access to information, ideas and works of
imagination for their social, educational, *cultural*, democratic and
economic well-being;...[38]

Although statement 2.3.2 follows immediately after a statement
specifically endorsing Article 19 of the UDHR, it clearly is a strong
affirmation of group economic, social, and cultural rights.

Beyond these documents, several scholars have pointed out the
imperative of those in the library and information professions to
work for social justice and human rights – including cultural rights.
Shiraz Durrani, the information worker originally from Kenya who
received his library science credentials in the U.K. and worked in
both his native Kenya and, later, Britain, has made passionate arguments that all libraries exist in a political, economic, and social
context and that libraries play a key role in "collecting, storing, and
disseminating knowledge and information relevant to the lives of
people."[39] He stresses that "relevance" is the key, otherwise libraries are neglecting their primary purpose. He also emphasizes that
for libraries to be relevant to the communities they serve, they
must not only have relevant content, but they must also provide
content in relevant media (e.g. audio-visual or oral resources) and
relevant languages to the communities in question. Durrani emphasizes that librarians and information workers would do well to
build off the already existing information structures in place in a
given community:

> History has shown that people do not wait for "outsiders" to
> come and satisfy their needs. A time comes in all societies when
> people take it upon themselves to satisfy their own needs, as it is
> a matter of their survival. People cannot wait while LIS workers

---

[38] International Federation of Library Associations, *IFLA Statues* (Hague:
IFLA, October 2008), 1-2, http://www.ifla.org/files/hq/ifla-statutes-
en.pdf (accessed May 31, 2009).

[39] Shiraz Durrani, "Information Relevance, Equality, and Material Security: The Kenyan Experience," *Library Review* 47:1 (1998): 20-25. Now
collected in Shiraz Durrani, *Information and Liberation: Writings on the Politics
of Information and Librarianship* (Duluth, MN: Library Juice Press, 2008), 61.
Citations are to the Library Juice edition.

spend years discussing how and what information to provide. They have developed their own information systems and will continue to do so. The question is whether the LIS profession is with people or not and also whether the profession is ready to work with the people in deciding what service they will have.[40]

Similar to Durrani, Toni Samek has documented ways in which library and information workers worldwide have developed social action strategies in working towards a 'critical librarianship' addressing human rights concerns including cultural rights. At the same time, Samek laments the tendency of the profession to focus more on process, technical, and managerial details rather than on the culture of critical librarianship necessary to better support core library values that encourage and promote active participation in the amelioration of social problems.[41] The voices that have emerged from African librarians over the past four decades have echoed these frustrations.

In addition to these scholars, Former IFLA President Kay Raseroka has drawn attention to the fact that the vision of the WSIS includes the following statement:[42]

> We, the representatives of the peoples of the world, assembled in Geneva from 10-12 December 2003 for the first phase of the World Summit on the Information Society, declare our common desire and commitment to build a people-centred, inclusive and development-oriented Information Society, where everyone can create, access, utilize and share information and knowledge, enabling individuals, communities and peoples to achieve their full potential in promoting their sustainable development and improving their quality of life, premised on the purposes and prin-

---

[40] Ibid., 66.
[41] Toni Samek, *Librarianship and Human Rights: A Twenty-First Century Guide* (Oxford: Chandos, 2007), 3-9.
[42] Kay Raseroka, "Access to Information and Knowledge," in *Human Rights in the Global Information Society*, ed. Rikke Frank Jørgensen (Cambridge, MA: MIT Press, 2006), 91-105.

ciples of the Charter of the United Nations and respecting fully
and upholding the Universal Declaration of Human Rights.[43]
While seeing this vision as an unqualified acceptance of the fundamental importance of human rights and cultural diversity, Raseroka
has argued that libraries must capitalize on the niche they occupy in
realizing the ideals of the information society by overcoming some
of their current challenges and finding more productive ways of
dealing with such cultural issues as orality, indigenous languages,
existing cultures of information exchange, and illiteracy.[44] Other
scholars have made compelling arguments for librarians' involvement in meeting human rights needs by examining the ways in
which other professions (doctors, lawyers, etc.) have shown their
commitment to advancing human rights, and arguing that librarians
have long been aware of the many ways that human rights values
intersect with the values of the profession. Due to this, they argue,
the library profession is bound to uphold its values whether or not
we as individuals consider ourselves "activists."[45] Given the definitions of cultural rights explored above and the imperative of librarians and information workers concern with cultural rights, I
now turn to an examination of these issues within the African context.

### History of Library Development in Sub-Saharan Africa

Sub-Saharan Africa, like other regions in the global South, has
been deeply affected by colonialism and imperialism. Neo-
colonialism disguised in economic, intellectual, and military interests continued in many African countries into the late 20th century.[46] Many would argue those same forces are still at work. The

---

[43] UN World Summit on the Information Society, *Declaration of Principles:
Building the Information Society: A Global Challenge in the New Millennium*,
WSIS-03/GENEVA/DOC/4-E 12, 12 December 2003.
http://www.un-documents.net/wsis-dop.htm (accessed May 31, 2009).
[44] Raseroka, "Access to Information," 92.
[45] Katharine J. Phenix and Kathleen de la Peña McCook, "Human Rights
and Librarians," *Reference and User Services Quarterly* 45:1 (2005): 23-26.
[46] For a discussion of the impact of neo-colonialism on culture, language,
and literature in Kenya, see Ngũgĩ Wa Thiong'o, *Moving the Center: The*

majority of political states which emerged from the colonial era have only been in existence since the late 1950s and early 1960s. Due to the powerful grip of colonial powers, and the young age of African nation states, the effects of colonialism and imperialism can still be seen across the continent. The history of library development and the library profession is no exception.[47] While there were known libraries on the African continent prior to colonialism,[48] oral tradition and the arts held the greatest responsibility for the preservation and transmission of knowledge and cultural values.[49] The colonial powers brought their European libraries with them, either to serve their populations exclusively, or to exert a type of intellectual control over the African populations. During this time, libraries were stocked with materials that colonial powers

---

*Struggle for Cultural Freedoms* (Oxford: James Currey, 1993); see also Ibid., *Decolonising the Mind: The Politics of Language in African Literature* (London: James Currey, 1986).

[47] For a detailed history of library development in Sub-Saharan Africa, see Sturges and Neill *Quiet Struggle*; see also Anthony Olden, *Libraries in Africa: Pioneers, Policies, Problems* (Lanham, MD: Scarecrow Press, 1995); see also Adolphe O. Amadi, "The Emergence of a Library Tradition in Pre- and Post-Colonial Africa," *International Library Review* 13 (1981): 65-72; for discussions of library development in Africa during the Cold War, see Amanda Laugesen, "'An Inalienable Right to Read': UNESCO's Promotion of a Universal Culture of Reading and Public Libraries and its Involvement in Africa, 1948-1968," *English in Africa* 35:1 (2008): 67-88; see also Mary Niles Maack, "Books and Libraries as Instruments of Cultural Diplomacy in Francophone Africa during the Cold War," *Libraries and Culture* 36:1 (2001): 58-86.

[48] Afeworki Paulos, "Library Resources, Knowledge Production, and Africa in the 21st Century," *International Information and Library Review* 40 (2008): 251-256. For example, the Library of Alexandria, monastic libraries in Ethiopia and Eritrea, and resource centers of learning in the Mali and Songhai empires.

[49] Ezekiel E. Kaungamno and Charles S. Ilomo, *Books Build Nations*, vol. 1. *Library Services in West and East Africa* (London: Transafrica Book Distributors, 1979); see also Amusi Odi, "The Colonial Origins of Library Development in Africa: Some Reflections on their Significance," *Libraries and Culture* 26:4 (1991): 594-604.

deemed important for the indigenous populations. Indigenous knowledge and local systems of information exchange were disparaged:

> Knowledge production under colonialism was not based on internal dynamism of a community, for indigenous knowledge production was excluded. Colonialism neither incorporated nor recognized indigenous knowledge. Indigenous knowledge was considered backward. Africans were told that progress and civilization could come only from ideas and knowledge generated outside Africa.[50]

To many Africans in the post-colonial nations, the image of the library was inherently connected with colonial rule. The libraries of the French, British, and Portuguese colonialists were often seen as propaganda tools for colonial administrators, representing one part of a multi-pronged effort to devastate the African worldview and subjugate the colonized into alignment with Western notions of reality. Collections across Sub-Saharan Africa from Dakar to Nairobi either reflected the "exalted nature of the colonial power's culture, the glory of its metropolis, or the primitiveness of the 'backward' peoples of Africa."[51]

The influence of Western notions of librarianship were evident not only in the physical facilities and materials found in the libraries themselves, but also in the ideology upon which African libraries were based. There was an underlying belief that the information needs and information seeking behavior of Africans were identical to those of library users in the global North and that the concept and philosophy of librarianship as practiced in the Anglo-American tradition could be simply imported to Africa without modifications. It was up to the African public to adapt themselves to this institution rather than the reverse.[52] There was also an assumption that the "need for information" among different communities (in a larger sense beyond specific information needs) would not differ in

---

[50] Paulos, "Library Resources, Knowledge Production," 251.
[51] Odi, "Colonial Origins of Library Development," 598.
[52] Kingo J. Mchombu, "Which Way African Librarianship?," *IFLA Journal* 17:1 (1991): 26-38.

any substantial way. Even the physical architecture of African libraries during the colonial and post-colonial period reflected the Western influence in such a way as to further alienate African communities. Great resources were spent to build monumental and attractive buildings while resources for services, training, and collections were neglected.[53] Collections in public libraries reflected a view of the world which was often of little relevance to the African communities in which they were housed. When large collections were developed for university libraries they often contained outdated materials with little or no academic or research value.[54] Even after independence many of the pioneer librarians were expatriates from the European continent.

The Western influence on the development of African libraries was also evident in the training of library professionals. African library schools have tended to base their curriculums on models from the global North, thus ignoring the unique information environment and needs of African communities.[55] Dependency relationships, reflected in the political, economic, social, and cultural relationships between the newly established Sub-Saharan countries and the former colonial powers, manifested in institutions throughout the new nations. Libraries provide an excellent example of the persistence of the colonial heritage after independence and the stifling effects of that relationship.[56]

The history of library development in Africa has also been deeply affected by a belief in the "problem" of the oral tradition and the ideology of librarianship as the preservation and documentation of the written word. The focus on the preservation of books and "knowledge" in archives ran counter to already existing Afri-

---

[53] Sturges and Neill, *Quiet Struggle*, 93-95.

[54] Mchombu, "Which Way African Librarianship?," 27.

[55] For further discussion on this see Mchombu, "Which Way African Librarianship?"; see also Martina A. Nwakoby, "Special Curricular Themes for Library Education in Nigeria," *International Library Review* 22:4 (1990): 213-224; see also Sturges and Neill, *Quiet Struggle*; see also Adolphe O. Amadi, *African Libraries: Western Tradition and Colonial Brainwashing* (Metuchen, NJ: Scarecrow, 1981).

[56] Sturges and Neill, *Quiet Struggle*, 93-95.

can systems of information and communication networking and the highly developed oral tradition. Oral tradition was one of the widespread elements of African culture that came under attack during the colonial period.[57] The labeling by Western colonials and neo-colonials of the oral tradition as a "problem" ignored the social, historical, and literary relevance of the tradition. Similarly, it severely limited the understanding of African cosmology, knowledge, and the intricate and rich communication systems which had developed over thousands of years.[58] Western colonialists, donors, and advisors to Africa viewed the written word and the book as the pinnacle of knowledge and went to great lengths to impose this view on others. Similarly, colonial languages were favored while indigenous ones were dismissed. The potential vision of an African library as a service or system to network existing community and local knowledge and in which individuals (e.g. elders, healers, priests, midwives, storytellers, or oral historians), artwork, musical compositions, realia, rituals, and other non-print based materials were recognized as "containers" of that knowledge was not recognized as a valid model by colonial librarians. These competing worldviews on information and communication manifested themselves in the discussions and literature on library development.

**The Competing Rhetoric of African Library Development**

In the period preceding the independence era and in the immediate post-independence age, the library literature from the global North was frequently marked by tones of paternalism and idealism with many discussions concluding that if Northern libraries, institutions, and associations adopted African libraries and assisted in the flow of information and resources from North to South, the problem of information poverty and stunted library development could

---

[57] H.O.M. Iwuji, "Librarianship and Oral Tradition in Africa," *International Library Review* 22:1 (1990): 53-59.
[58] Sturges and Neill, *Quiet Struggle*, 52-54; see also Anaba A. Alemna, *Issues in African Librarianship* (Kaneshie, Accra: Type Co., 1996), 9-15; see also Raseroka, "Access to Information," 92-93.

be alleviated.[59] Expatriate librarians did a great deal to set the course of library development in Africa during this time. While they came with the best intentions and many recognized and expressed awareness of the need to develop systems and services that could be well-integrated with the unique social, political, and cultural circumstances of their host communities, these intentions did not manifest.[60] Rather than a meaningful philosophical debate on the construct of the library ideal and information provision, this first batch of expatriate librarians instead attempted to put into place the same systems and patterns of library bureaucracy that existed in their countries of origin.[61]

The discourse of paternalism and idealism is everywhere evident in the library literature of this time. One excellent example comes from Wilfred John Plumbe,[62] one of the most distinguished British expatriate librarians, who had worked in many parts of the colonial world. In his introduction to the Fall 1959 edition of the journal *Library Trends*, which focused on "Current Trends in Newly Developing Countries," Plumbe displays the paternalism and the world-view these expatriate librarians brought with them to their work:

> The masses of Asia, Africa, the Middle East, and Latin America may not yet realize how libraries can change their lives but there is increasing awareness by educationists, politicians, scientists, and all species of administrators, that library services in academic institutions, schools, research organizations, and to the community at large, are fundamental to most other activities and provide the basis for beneficial change. This increasing acceptance

---

[59] Lor and Britz, "Knowledge Production," 61-62. See the 1980 publication of the report *Many Voices, One World* (also known as the McBride Report) by the International Commission for the Study of Communication Problems as a significant turning point in an attitude change toward the issue.

[60] Sturges and Neill, *Quiet Struggle*, 88-89.

[61] For detailed examples of the results of this "alien implant" see Sturges and Neill, *Quiet Struggle*, 88-116.

[62] See Wilfred J. Plumbe, *Tropical Librarianship* (Metuchen, N.J.: Scarecrow Press, 1987) for a full look at his ideas concerning library development in the Global South.

of "the library idea" in newly developing territories is the most important general trend that may be discerned.[63]

Plumbe goes on to appreciate the international style of library architecture made possible by modern concrete technology. He also stresses the importance of visiting librarians and experts to these countries, made possible by UNESCO and other agencies, to develop the library systems and help in setting up schools of librarianship where "high standards should be achieved."[64]

> Growing help from "outside" constitutes a clear trend in development. The United States Information Service and British Council libraries, although small and limited in scope, have greatly exceeded their ambassadorial and propagandist functions, and appreciation of them is worldwide.[65]

Plumbe, in discussing how local authorities must be convinced of the importance of official support for the libraries, explains:

> But in the heart of Africa...where enlightened public administration may not be taken for granted, it is still most difficult, sometimes, to establish adequate standards of book provision, library buildings, staffing, and personal service; and it is here that advice and solid financial aid from "outside" have been, and in future can be, invaluable.[66]

To his credit, Plumbe, unlike some of his compatriots, acknowledged that publications must be made available in the local languages otherwise books would remain on the shelves and readers would be frustrated; however, he indicated that this was a problem to be considered only in those countries which had not adopted an official European language. It was implied that for those postcolonial countries which had adopted an official European language, there was no longer a problem. No mention or recognition of the importance of the oral tradition or the existing patterns of communication and information transfer already used by the com-

---

[63] Wilfred J. Plumbe, "Introduction," *Library Trends* 8:2 (1959): 126.
[64] Ibid., 127.
[65] Ibid., 127.
[66] Ibid., 127.

munities was given. Plumbe's final and concluding statements display the paternalism and missionary zeal that is found in much of the writing by Northern authors on African libraries during this era:

> The human story behind all this effort will never be told, or it will be titrated into statistics. It is a small, not very noticeable, part of the saga in social history through which we are living. It has been epitomized by a tribal African who once remarked to the present writer: "The day of the spear has gone; the day of the book has come."[67]

Clearly, the mindset commonly held amongst those early librarians was that the European had brought the book and thus "civilization" to the illiterate savages on the great continent.

A compatriot of Plumbe's, Bernard I. Palmer, writing also in the 1959 issue of *Library Trends*, describes the education and training of librarians in the British Commonwealth Countries and exemplifies the same rhetoric:

> Now, "a library is a growing organism," and the appointment of a librarian, indigenous or from overseas, is only the first step towards the future staffing of the library. The second step is the recruitment of local assistance. Frequently this takes the form of a clerk or clerks, who must be instructed in the elements of library work. The better ones respond to this treatment, and since all librarians are educators the intern-training system for the specific library's use widens in scope and soon the librarian is imparting his full knowledge to his staff, and is guiding them in their reading.[68]

Palmer goes on to commend the expatriate librarians for their role in educating the local population in the colonial mindset:

> The British Council librarians have done a magnificent job of training, with little or no resources at their command, and have frequently been responsible for the first appearance of local

---

[67] Ibid., 129.
[68] Bernard I. Palmer, "Education and Training of Librarians in the Newly Developing British Commonwealth Countries," *Library Trends* 8:2 (1959): 232.

people on the Library Association's Register of chartered librarians. In furthering knowledge of the British way of life, no group
in the community is more worth the expenditure of time and
money than librarians, to whom adults turn freely for help and
advice all their lives.[69]

These passages again exemplify the attitudes of the times, that the
colonial powers of the North were the bringers of knowledge, order, and civilization through the vehicle of library development.

While I will demonstrate later in the chapter that in many ways
there has been a shift in tone from Northern information workers
concerning African libraries, in some senses "the more things
change, the more they stay the same." Writing much later in the
20th century, G.G. Chowdhury,[70] discussing the changes in Africa's
ICT environment, sounds eerily familiar:

> Thanks to the many donor agencies and international organiza-
> tions, the face of Africa's information and communication sce-
> nario has been changing to keep pace with the global develop-
> ments, and soon Africa will be an active participant in the Global
> Information Infrastructure and be able to drive on the Super-
> highway.[71]

To his credit, Chowdhury recognizes and stresses the importance
of such cultural factors as resources in local languages and the
building of local information resources so that indigenous information content is available; however, his conclusion is similar to
Plumbe's in 1959 – outside aid from experts who can properly
train, equip and enlighten the population are the only hope for advancement in the African information environment.

---

[69] Ibid., 232.

[70] G.G. Chowdhury is a distinguished expatriate faculty member who has
served at the School of Information Studies for Africa (SISA) and is
author of many books and articles on information retrieval, digital resources, and librarianship.

[71] G.G. Chowdhury, "The Changing Face of Africa's Information and
Communication Scenario," *International Information and Library Review* 30
(1998): 20-1.

## Voices from the Continent

While Northern librarians wrote on African libraries in this manner, a new approach to the view and concept of the library began to emerge from within the continent. Ironically, the roots of this competing rhetoric can be seen in the debate between the two expatriate librarians Wilfred Plumbe, mentioned above, and Ronald Benge, through an exchange of letters in the *Library Association Record*.[72] Plumbe had argued that the Library Association of the U.K. should adapt its professional education syllabus to be more sensitive to the needs of overseas librarians. In proposing this, however, he did not see any need to change the underlying philosophical foundations of the U.K. library service, which he believed to be transcendent of national boundaries. Benge, in contrast, expressed his belief that Plumbe's focus on physical, environmental, and geographic factors affecting library development in Africa missed much of the point. Rather, Benge recognized that Africa had its own social and cultural values and he thus concluded that librarianship in Africa should build and draw inspiration from those values.[73] He went on to flesh out those ideas in his book *Cultural Crisis and Libraries in the Third World*.[74] African librarians quickly joined their voices into this debate and began to express more and more frustration with the hegemonic influence of Northern dominated modes of thought concerning library development. They drew attention to the fact that this model ignored important cultural aspects including already existing patterns of information and knowledge transfer, local languages, social structures, and the vitality of the oral tradition. Although this rhetoric was not couched in the language of human rights (or cultural rights), the relationship is clearly visible.

Perhaps the strongest example of this anti-Northern and hegemonic tradition can be found in Adolphe Amadi's book *Afri-*

---

[72] Sturges and Neill, *Quiet Struggle*, 128-129.
[73] Ibid., 129.
[74] Ronald C. Benge, *Cultural Crisis and Libraries in the Third World* (London: Clive Bingley, 1979).

*can Libraries: Western Tradition and Colonial Brainwashing.*[75] Amadi focused his work on the negative effects and history of the colonial
influence on the African librarian and made a strong case for the
need for a radically different approach. Benge and Amadi laid the
groundwork for what was to become known as "African Librarianship." Younger African librarians adopted this approach and rhetoric which highlighted the need for an African-centric model of library development focused on existing cultural and social values
and needs within African communities. These younger librarians
often faced stiff resistance as they sought to bring down the old
paradigm.[76] While the rhetoric did not specifically address the issues as human rights concerns, the authors framed the discussion
within an anti-colonial and anti-imperialism discourse that is currently recognized as a key part of the development of a global human rights movement. Today this situation has shifted and we see
more awareness of issues related to models of African library development within a human rights context. For example, the theme
of the 2010 conference of the Standing Conference of Eastern,
Central and Southern Africa Library and Information Associations
(SCECSAL) is "Enhancing Democracy and Good Governance
through Effective Information and Knowledge Services" and contains several sub-themes specifically addressing individual human
rights or human rights as an umbrella concept.[77]

Another seminal work in this area was an article published by
K.J. Mchombu, a training officer with the Tanzania National Library Service at the time, in the journal *Libri* in 1982 entitled *On the
Librarianship of Poverty*. Mchombu argued that the conditions of
poverty must be the base on which any discussion of information
work in under-developed countries must be anchored. He elabo-

---

[75] Adolphe O. Amadi, *African Libraries: Western Tradition and Colonial Brainwashing* (Metuchen, NJ: Scarecrow, 1981).

[76] Sturges and Neill, *Quiet Struggle*, 130.

[77] Botswana Library Association, "SCECSAL XIX Conference: XIXth
Standing Conference of Eastern, Central and Southern Africa Library and
Information Associations (SCECSAL) 7th - 10th September 2010, Gaborone, Botswana," http://www.scecsal.org/conferences/2010/2010.html
(accessed September 28, 2009).

rated four principles he felt were necessary in order to make information work in developing countries socially relevant:

1. That the chief factor determining Information work in developing countries should be poverty rather than affluence.

2. That Information work in developing countries differs markedly from Information work in developed countries.

3. That it is possible to gather a body of knowledge on how best to meet this challenge.

4. That Information workers must play an active role in the process of socio-economic development.[78]

Mchombu's article became a rallying cry and an agenda for a whole generation of African librarians. Mchombu pointed out that scholars in other areas, such as economics, sociology, political science, and education had done much work in developing a theoretical base for their professions relevant to underdeveloped countries. "With careful interdisciplinary comparative studies, we could learn a lot that would be of great value in this undertaking – if only we could for a moment think beyond our hallowed DDC's, Sears Lists, and cataloguing rules."[79] In sharp contrast to Plumbe and Palmer, Mchombu lamented the influence of the global North and the previous colonial powers on the training of library and information staff:

> Most of the staff holding senior positions in underdeveloped countries have been trained on a background of Information work as practiced in industrialized countries. Not unexpectedly, the prevailing attitude is that this is the way in which users should behave, and the way in which Information services operate. My belief, already stated, is that this is an erroneous view of things because the lavish standards of service that exist in a typical developed country are impossible to maintain in a poor country, unless the objective is to provide an Information service for the fortunate few rather than the majority of mankind in devel-

---

[78] Kingo J. Mchombu, "On the Librarianship of Poverty," *Libri* 32:3 (1982): 241.
[79] Ibid., 244.

oping societies. Indeed, this does, sadly, appear to be the unstated objective of many an Information service in developing countries. After more than 15 years of existence, and expenditure of millions of shillings, many public Library systems have not yet succeeded in serving more than 1% of the population in their areas.[80]

After discussing at length the existing social factors and their implications for information workers, Mchombu concluded "The scarcity of resources must be reflected by: the pattern of Information services; the role of Information Workers; the way that Information Services are adapted to the locality concerned and the active participation of Information Workers in national development."[81] He emphasized that information services in developing countries should not follow standards blindly copied from developed countries and that information workers need to develop an aggressive attitude and participate fully in the social struggle for national development. He concluded his manifesto unequivocally with the statement "The conclusion is that Information Workers must look for solutions to their problems within their own societies rather than depending on foreign aid."[82]

While Amadi and Mchombu's writings serve as key examples of the early rhetoric of African librarianship, many African librarians and information workers continued to carry forth this cry and agenda throughout the second half of the twentieth century. Some African librarians focused their writing on the need for greater research on community needs and existing patterns of information transfer than the Anglo-English librarian model allowed.[83] Others,

---

[80] Ibid., 245-246.

[81] Ibid., 250.

[82] Ibid., 250.

[83] For discussions on Nigerian agricultural and public libraries during this time, see Emmanuel N.O. Adimorah, "An Overview of the State of Information Provision to Rural Communities in Anglophone West Africa," in *Seminar on Information Provision to Rural Communities in Africa: Proceedings of the Seminar held in Gaborone, Botswana, 22-25 June 1994*, ed. Eve Johansson (Uppsla, Sweden: Uppsla University Library, 1995), 80-81; see also Emmanuel N.O. Adimorah, "Rural Community Information Systems and

like B. Olabimpe Aboyade, stressed that information services should repackage information into forms culturally and socially acceptable by the local population.[84] Still others, such as Anaba A. Alemna from Ghana, emphasized the importance of utilizing the oral tradition as an information resource in African libraries.[85] Many stressed the importance of changing the library model inherited by the colonial powers to recognize the information needs and abilities of non-literates.[86] Several African librarians addressed the issues of availability of resources in local African languages. As post-independence African nations struggled to come up with viable language policies, some kept the colonial language in an attempt to avoid conflict between ethnic groups and to open up the possibility of advancement in the world theater.[87] Others choose to

---

Culture in Africa," *Resource Sharing and Information Networks* 8:2 (1993): 91-118; see also L.O. Aina, "Information for Successful Agriculture," *Third World Libraries* 2:1 (1991): 49-53; for discussion of research in information seeking behaviors in Zambia, see Andrew M. Kaniki, "Information Seeking and Information Providers among Zambian Farmers," *Libri* 41 (1991): 147-64; for discussion of information needs and existing patterns of exchange in Malawi, see Kingo J. Mchombu, "Information Needs for Rural Development: The Case Study of Malawi," *African Journal of Library, Archives, and Information Science* 2:1 (1992): 17-32.

[84] B. Olabimpe Aboyade, "Communications Potentials of the Library for Non-Literates: An Experiment in Providing Information Services in a Rural Setting," *Libri* 34:3 (1984): 243-62.

[85] Anaba A. Alemna, "Towards a New Emphasis on Oral Tradition as an Information Source in African Libraries," *Journal of Documentation* 48:4 (1992): 422-429; see also Iwuji, "Librarianship and Oral Tradition in Africa"; see also Raphael Ndiaye, "Oral Culture and Libraries," *IFLA Journal* 14:1 (1988): 40-46.

[86] Gboyega Banjo, "Libraries and Cultural Heritage in Africa," *IFLA Journal* 24 (1998): 228-232; see also Fatogoma Diakite, "The Dissemination of Information in a Rural Environment: The Public Library Services and the Rural Audio Libraries of Mali," in *Seminar on Information Provision* (see note 82), 71-79.

[87] Mamoud Akanni Igue and Raphael Windali N'Oueni, "The Politics of Language in Benin," in *African Languages, Development, and the State*, ed. Richard Fardon and Graham Furniss (London: Routledge, 1994), 55-61; see also John Povey, "Language Planning in Africa," *Vox: The Journal of the*

establish an African language as their national language for school-
ing and politics.[88] A few tried to provide education in a large variety
of languages while also teaching and using a national or colonial
language.[89] As African authors such as Kenyan author Ngũgĩ wa
Thiong'o made strong arguments and impassioned pleas for
authors to use indigenous languages in their writing,[90] similarly,
African librarians made arguments that written resources in local
languages must be found in African libraries if they are truly to
have relevance to the local community and culture.[91]

**Changes in the Debate**

As the closing of the twentieth century grew near, more librarian and information workers from the Northern countries were
recognizing the importance of the model of African librarianship
being argued for vehemently by voices from within the continent,
and several Northern authors broke ranks with the colonial past to
endorse the vision being presented by their African colleagues. Diana Rosenberg, in looking at rural libraries and information provision, raised important issues of sustainability which built off of
Mchombu's earlier concerns and ideas.[92] Alfred Kagan argued that

---

*Australian Advisory Council on Languages and Multicultural Education* 5 (1991):
72-75.

[88] Regina Mezei, "Somali Language and Literacy," *Language Problems and
Language Planning* 13:3 (1989): 211-223; see also Jeff Unsicker, "Tanzania's
Literacy Campaign in Historical-Structural Perspective," in *National Literacy Campaigns: Historical and Comparative Perspectives*, ed. Robert F. Arnove
and Harvey J. Graff (New York: Plenum, 1987), 219-244.

[89] F. Niyi Akinnaso and Isaac A. Ogunbiyi, "The Place of Arabic in Language Education and Language Planning in Nigeria," *Language Problems and
Language Planning*, 14:1 (1990): 1-19.

[90] Ngũgĩ Wa Thiong'o, *Moving the Center*; see also Ibid., *Decolonising the
Mind*.

[91] Shiraz Durrani, "Information Relevance, Equality," 63-64.

[92] Diana Rosenberg, "Can Libraries in Africa Ever be Sustainable?," *Infor-
mation Development* 10 (1994): 247-251; see also Ibid., "Imposing Libraries:
The Establishment of National Public Library Services in Africa, with
Particular Reference to Kenya," *Third World Libraries* 4:1 (1993): 35-44; see

one of the three functions of the African rural library was to serve as centers for community, education, and culture.[93] B.J. Mostert, in discussing public library services in South Africa, explored the implications and results of information service provision in rural areas that were ill-matched to their environment and concluded that community library services should not be imposed from outside the community nor should they be based on the Western concept of the library.[94] Perhaps most dramatically, Peter Lor, a South African librarian of European heritage, set out principles for a reformed South African librarianship which built off Mchombu's call for the librarianship of poverty. These principles included:

1. Libraries try to operate at too high a level, and this level should be lowered, without ceasing to strive after excellence.

2. Librarians should commit themselves to the aspirations and values of the communities they serve.

3. There should not be discrimination against users on the basis of literacy.

4. Libraries should give a much higher priority to communication than to organization.

5. Librarians should accept that community information resources have a higher claim on funding than have sophisticated information services.[95]

Sturges and Neill, in responding to Lor, answered that a completely new paradigm was needed, one which shifted from an emphasis on

---

also Ibid., "Rural Community Resource Centres: A Sustainable Option for Africa?," *Information Development* 9:1/2 (1993): 29-35.

[93] Alfred Kagan, "Literacy, Libraries, and Underdevelopment - with Special Attention to Tanzania," *Africana Journal* 13:1/4 (1982): 1-23.

[94] B.J. Mostert, "Community Libraries: The Concept and its Application - with Particular Reference to a South African Community Library System," *International Information and Library Review* 30 (1998): 71-76.

[95] Peter Johan Lor, "Africanisation of South African Libraries: A Response to Some Recent Literature" (paper, Info Africa Nova Conference, Pretoria, May 4, 1993) cited in Sturges and Neill, *Quiet Struggle*, 135.

libraries to "total information provision." They specified that the
new paradigm of information service in Africa must be based on:

1. Financial realism

2. Self-reliance

3. Sustainability

4. Democracy

5. Responsiveness

6. Communication[96]

By democracy, the authors meant that this principle is "a far reach-
ing requirement for service to the whole of the people, rather than
just to minorities who might be literate, articulate, influential, geo-
graphically accessible or, even, able to pay."[97] In a bold statement,
quite different from many of their Northern colleagues in the Anglo-American tradition, Sturges and Neill echoed the call of many
of the African authors cited earlier in this chapter:

> Africa's libraries and other information institutions urgently need
> to break the dependence on Northern values which continues to
> retard their development. Dependence is as much a psychologi-
> cal phenomenon as an economic one. Indeed, economic chains
> do not always bind as strongly at those of the mind. To break
> away from an unwanted dependence is, therefore, not at all easy.
> What is more, in this case it may, in the short term, increase the
> poverty that afflicts African information institutions. To be poor
> is bad, but to be locked into relationships that limit the options
> for breaking out of that poverty is worse. These relationships
> can be changed.
>
> It is essential for Africa's library and information community to
> struggle to avoid dependence on international publishing and
> bookselling companies, to ensure that donor agencies do not set
> the parameters of what can be done by the nature of the assis-
> tance they give, or that telecommunication and computer tech-
> nology do not create patterns of information flow incompatible

---

[96] Sturges and Neill, *Quiet Struggle*, 136-40.
[97] Ibid., 139.

with developing country aims. Even more important than this, however, is the need to combat the psychological dependence which is nurtured by modes of thought and philosophies developed in other parts of the world, where both information needs and the resources to meet them are quite different. The imported attitudes and preconceptions of librarianship which dominate in Africa at present both permit and encourage the ways in which this dependency manifests itself.[98]

The roots of the debate had spread wide and far. At the close of the first decade of the twenty-first century, after witnessing the changes of increased globalization, the declaration of the Millennium Development Goals, the development and expansion of new ICTs, the open source and open access movements, the holding of the WSIS, and the global financial crisis, where does the status of this rhetorical debate stand? What new rhetoric and models for African libraries and African information provision are being promoted and to what extent do they address the cultural rights discussed at the beginning of this chapter?

**Current Rhetoric and the State of Cultural Rights in African Information Work**

In many ways the rhetorical debate between the model of librarianship from the global North and the distinctly different paradigm of "African Librarianship" is still actively taking place. The voices of African librarians and information workers repeat many of the earlier concerns from thirty years ago; however, there is a new emphasis on the role of ICTs and the questions related to their use concerning culture, development, and democracy. At the same time, the voices from Northern librarians and organizations represent a diverse discourse with some continuing strongly in the neocolonial tradition and others building off the more radical sentiments expressed by Lor and Sturges and Neill in the previous section.

Durrani, writing in 2006 about the Progressive African Librarian and Information Activists Group (PALIAct), describes how this group of African librarians and information workers was re-

---

[98] Ibid., 114.

energized during IFLA's 2002 meeting when participants at the
Africa Regional Section came to the agreement that "African Librarianship needs to liberate itself from the colonial-imperialist
mould."[99] As we see, it's a different millennium but the same cry
for change can be heard. Durrani explains that PALIAct provides a
vision for a people-oriented information service; works towards
providing an anti-imperialist and Pan African world outlook among
information workers; seeks to set up alternative information services in partnership with the users; and aims to form partnerships
with progressive information and other workers within Africa and
overseas.[100] PALIAct centers are being piloted in Kenya and
Ghana. While the strengths of the centers have been the enthusi-
asm of those individuals and communities involved, Durrani laments that the public library structures in the regions have not actively supported PALIAct because they are marginalized themselves and don't have the financial or other resources necessary to
support their own services, much less collaborate or support the
PALIAct vision. Durrani also describes a lack of political will from
the African governments and regional organizations in the areas.
New era, familiar problems.

Raseroka's recent writing in relation to the WSIS addresses the
challenges she feels that libraries need to overcome if they are to
truly assist in realizing the ideals of the WSIS vision statement. Libraries must find more productive approaches to working with
cultural issues such as orality, indigenous languages, and the existing cultures of information exchange. They must also find appropriate cultural mechanisms for aiding literacy development and a
reading culture if there is to truly be an inclusive information society.[101] As with other African librarians and information workers
writing today, Raseroka's rhetoric has changed to incorporate the
new challenges and opportunities offered by ICTs. Raseroka emphasizes the paradox inherent in this issue. While ICTs have the

---

[99] Shiraz Durrani, "Progressive Librarianship in Africa: the PALIAct
Story," *Focus on International Library and Information Work* 37:1 (2006): 4-8.
Now collected in Shiraz Durrani, *Information and Liberation* (see note 39).
[100] Ibid., 295.
[101] Raseroka, "Access to Information and Knowledge," 91-92.

potential to enable people to produce, record, process, and disseminate information, and to integrate orality and visuality (non-
text communication), ICTs must be considered in the context of
the existing conditions and influences that have created the current
information divide. ICTs represent an "opportunity for
empowerment of communities to share and contribute their stories
and for librarians to facilitate the capture, preservation, and dissemination of local information through various communication
technologies, subject to applicable intellectual property rights."[102]
However, Raseroka states clearly this admonition:

> In the disadvantageous environment occupied by the majority of
> people who live in developing countries, and the urban poor in
> developed countries, the lack of access to ICT is the first hurdle.
> Where it is accessible, the cost of use and the skills needed for
> ICT use are barriers. The introduction of ICTs in this environ-
> ment therefore has a potential to amplify existing inequalities.[103]

Additionally Raseroka, unlike several of her African colleagues who
exalt existing information provision structures rooted in local cultures, points to their potential tyranny:

> The fundamental challenge in developing an information society
> in a generalized African culture is that there is already an infor-
> mation society model of hierarchy, age, and gender prescription
> that is opposed to the principles of human rights on freedom of
> access to information and freedom of expression. Unless this
> fundamental approach to information access and communica-
> tion within traditional developing societies is addressed, the en-
> visaged information society will be a mirage for millions who
> cling to traditions and indigenous cultures of information-
> sharing within prescribed systems.[104]

In making this connection, Raseroka points to the paradox and
difficulty concerning cultural rights mentioned by Eide earlier in
this chapter. The manifestations of cultural rights, while a benefit
to some, can also create a prison for others, unless the individual

---

[102] Ibid., 97.
[103] Ibid., 97.
[104] Ibid., 100.

truly has the opportunity to participate in that cultural life that is most pertinent to him or her. Raseroka's observations, when examined within the light of Eide's comments, point to the crucial importance of a model of African librarianship where the more inclusive reading of cultural rights presented in the ICESCR's Article 15, the right "to take part in cultural life," is vital. This broader reading recognizes that there are many cultures within one community, rather than *the* implied one cultural life of *the* community as stated in the UDHR's Article 27. It also accepts that the individual has the right to choose which cultural life of the community is most pertinent to him or her. With this broader reading, libraries and information workers must seek ways to provide spaces where all cultural traditions in the community, and in an individual, are equally valued and represented if they are to truly fulfill their role in meeting human rights obligations.

As a concrete example of a new library/information model, Raseroka has described a project in Botswana whose aim is to "nurture local content creation through the breakdown of cultural barriers to intergenerational information expression/access. It seeks to encourage elders to be open to answering children's questions and to nurture children's understanding that they are permitted to ask questions and to develop their rights and duties of asking questions, within the cultural norms."[105] The elders involved share local culture stories in their mother tongue. The project also involves the use of ICTs in processing and posting the stories. Computers and software have been provided in partnership with UNICEF. In discussing the various actors and negotiations that took place for this project to work, Raseroka emphasizes that this effort has represented holistic engagement between the librarians working with communities. However, other earlier writers might argue that this still represents a dependency model (relying on ICTs from UNICEF) and a disrespect for local cultural tradition by the fact that a goal of the program is for cultural barriers to be "broken down." Raseroka puts emphasis on the factors she feels must be in place if ICTs are going to be the tools for building a fair and just

---

[105] Ibid., 100.

society claimed by so many. Among these factors are: a respect for the principles of the UDHR (including recognition of cultural pluralism); that all people are "empowered to communicate in their own voice and language, and to generate local content for their own use and exchange"; and the principles of fair and equal exchange of information resources. Without these factors, Raseroka does not see a radically different reality than that which has plagued the African information environment in the past, with technologically advanced and economically powerful nations owning and manipulating the intended information society.[106]

It is clear that the factors highlighted by Raseroka must be present if a new model of African information work is going to firmly break the bonds of the colonial past. While there are many examples of how the principles of fair and equal exchange of information are currently being ignored, there is also growing evidence that new movements such as the open source and open access movements and indigenous knowledge management philosophies are propelling African information work towards equity. The question remains however, can these new movements be strong enough and widespread enough to combat the hegemonic forces of global capitalism and the resulting cultural influences of language and commodification?

Related to this, other African information workers writing in the first decade of the 21st century have built on the concerns of earlier librarians by emphasizing the importance, challenges, and dilemmas of the documentation and communication of indigenous knowledge. Jabulani Sithole points out the individualistic nature of indigenous knowledge (from grandparent or parent to child) and the concept of "knowledge as power" in which knowledge is a source of status and income and is thus guarded jealously and cannot be easily shared.[107] This raises difficulties for libraries to document and disseminate this cultural knowledge. Sithole also explores the complex issues of intellectual property rights with regards to

---

[106] Ibid., 103
[107] Jabulani Sithole, "The Challenges Faced by African Libraries and Information Centres in Documenting and Preserving Indigenous Knowledge," *IFLA Journal* 33:2: 122.

indigenous knowledge. In contrast with earlier African librarians, Sithole and some of his colleagues elaborate more on the complex issues raised with the promotion of cultural rights such as use of indigenous knowledge. For the earlier librarians, the documentation and communication of indigenous knowledge was an ideal and goal for the reformed "African librarianship," whereas, for today's librarians, it is a reality with its own nuances, challenges, complexities, and a host of ethical issues.

The signs of paternalism and missionary zeal that manifested in the earlier writings from librarians of the global North are still evident today. The difference, however, is that there is more of a generalized recognition and acceptance of certain aspects of cultural rights where often none existed before. For example, Betsie Greyling, the systems librarian at eThekwini Municipal Library in Durban, South Africa has written about a model developed for public libraries in South Africa whereby the public libraries engage the community in establishing a digital library of indigenous knowledge. In this model, community workers collect oral and visual materials, community members are taught how to add materials to the Internet at the library, the library acts as moderator and custodian (rather than owners) of the indigenous knowledge resource, and the community in partnership with the library is a key element. While this innovative approach appears overall to be community focused and favoring cultural rights, there is a paternalistic tone to the description of the foreseen benefits:

> A website of local indigenous knowledge will provide information about local technologies and culture. Improved digital skills will result in economic empowerment of communities and progress in poverty alleviation. Knowledge provision will enable behavior changes and informed decision making, as well as promoting the creation of new knowledge within the community. It will stimulate innovative thinking, aid learning and promote indigenous technologies. Formal and informal knowledge levels in the community will be enhanced, leading to an informed society.

Ultimately a culture of knowledge sharing between community members will improve social cohesion in the community.[108] In addition to echoing earlier sentiments of ex-colonial librarians, these statements diminish the fact that knowledge sharing and new knowledge creation are already a part of the community. While the creation of the website of local indigenous knowledge with the community's participation is a worthwhile goal for an African library seeking to be more relevant to the community and achieve the objectives above, a successful library would also create spaces and networks to expand existing knowledge transfers already taking place within the community. These might take the form of community forums, discussion groups, festivals, demonstrations of local agricultural or manufacturing techniques, or musical performances.

Similarly, another librarian from the Anglo-American tradition, Valeda F. Dent Goodman, has recently reported on impact studies in current rural village libraries in Ghana and Burkina Faso. The libraries were started in 2001 by the Friends of African Village Libraries, an organization based in California. The qualitative and quantitative data was gathered by researchers from the USA and Germany in separate studies conducted between 2004 and 2007.[109] Several elements of the libraries' operation show a recognition for cultural rights, such as materials relevant to the community in local languages and the importance of the librarian as a member of the community. Yet, the old model still remains. Focus groups and individual interviews played a role in the qualitative data gathering. Several of the questions in the survey are leading questions such as "Do you think having the library in the community has improved your quality of life? How?" and "Do books help you cope with the day-to-day problems, for example, health-related, job-related, par-

---

[108] Betsie Greyling, "A Model for Community Participation in African Libraries to Preserve Indigenous Knowledge," *Information Studies* 14:2 (2008): 81-82.
[109] Valeda F. Dent Goodman, "Rural Library Services: Historical Development and Modern-Day Examples from West Africa," *New Library World* 109:11/12 (2008): 519.

enting, etc."[110] Goodman concludes, based on the data gathered, that these rural libraries are prime examples of how "an institution that has historically been ineffective for the majority of residents in many African countries – in this case, the public library – can in fact be crafted to serve a variety of needs of those in rural areas"[111] and "The importance of supporting the newly literate and the development of reading cultures in rural areas cannot be overstated. This is best accomplished with local community collaborations that provide access to reading materials and other services while advancing respect for local languages, cultures, and practices."[112] While cultural elements such as languages, cultural practices, and community connections are clearly given some attention, the overall impression of this project is one in which an outside group has created the service and is then creating the paradigm with which to evaluate it. There may be much more cultural sensitivity than previous models in the immediate post-colonial era but the idea of "cultural rights" as elaborated by scholars on cultural rights as well as the more "radical" librarians, both African and Anglo-American, cited earlier does not appear to be present in this type of example. It is a far cry from the radical approaches advocated and discussed earlier by Mchombu, Amadi, Lor, and Sturges and Neill.

Despite the two examples above, several librarians from the global North or from European heritage have continued to elaborate on the ideas of the radicals and call for a different vision for African libraries, one that emphasizes the financial realities of African countries and societies, the oral means of information sharing, promotion of community context above all other, active rather than passive information sharing, and promotion of indigenous production of knowledge rather than information coming solely from publishers outside of Africa.[113] Johannes J. Britz and Lor have

---

[110] Ibid., 524.

[111] Ibid., 529.

[112] Ibid., 530.

[113] Diana Rosenberg, "Giving Journals Published in Africa a Presence on the Web: The African Journals Online Project," *The Serials Librarian* 37:3 (2000): 71-82; see also Jacques C. du Plessis, "'From Food Silos to Com-

written eloquently on the ethical dimensions of the "global information society" and some of the current elements that are "morally
wrong," including unfair intellectual property right regimes –
specifically toward the developing countries; unfair exploitation and
misappropriation of indigenous knowledge and artifacts; and the
imbalance of north-south and south-north flow of information.[114]
Britz and Lor have identified three core principles and seven categories of justice they propose can be used as the moral cornerstone
for facing the ethical challenges of the global Information Society.
Although much of their writing relates to access issues more commonly associated with Article 19 of the UDHR, the authors have
strong statements in favor of cultural rights and group rights to
self-determination. Similarly, Rafael Capurro, another information
worker from the global North, in writing of information ethics and
Africa, has looked deeply at both the impact of ICTs on African
societies and cultures from a philosophical perspective and the
meaning of cultural and collective memory. Capurro reminds both
Northern and African audiences:

> The retrieving of African cultural memory in the field of infor-
> mation and communication is a main challenge for information
> ethics. It requires awareness of the different strategies of social
> inclusion and exclusion in the history of African societies, in-
> cluding such traumatic experiences as slavery and apartheid in-
> terpreted under this perspective. With the emergence of the In-
> ternet, the most recent expression of this challenge with regard
> to the new information and communication technologies is be-
> ing discussed under the heading of the digital divide. But much
> more is involved than just access to and use of this medium, par-
> ticularly if all other forms of social exclusion, manipulation, ex-
> ploitation, and annihilation of human beings are left out of the

---

munity Kitchens' - Retooling African Libraries," *International Information
and Library Review* 40 (2008): 43-51.
[114] Johannes J. Britz, "Making the Global Information Society Good: A
Social Justice Perspective on the Ethical Dimensions of the Global Information Society," *Journal of the American Society for Information Science and
Technology* 5:7 (2008): 1173; see also Peter Johan Lor and Johannes Britz,
"Knowledge Production from an African Perspective".

discussion by reducing the digital divide to merely a technical problem.[115]

Capurro, Britz, Lor and other more recent librarians and information workers from the global North reveal that there has been a change in the rhetoric from outside African communities. While the colonial legacy lives on in information work and discourse, there has also been a shift, at least in awareness, if not always in practice.

### Conclusion: The Importance of Cultural Rights and Library and Information Development in Sub-Saharan Africa

As an American information worker who came to the field because of my experiences working in education and literacy in a rural area of the Central African Republic (C.A.R.) where I was called upon by the local community to help develop a library, I have seen first hand how good intentions can fail and even sometimes do harm. Because of this I am deeply aware that the discourse of library development in Africa is not just an issue of rhetoric. Rather, it can have a profound impact on lives and communities. The voices of African librarians calling for a new vision of information work on the continent is beginning to make an impact on librarians and information workers in the global North. The question remains however, what substantial change will have occurred when we look back from fifty years down the road? As African and non-African librarians seek to incorporate cultural rights into information work, other issues will need to be negotiated and resolved, such as Raseroka's and Eide's points concerning the tension between cultural models of hierarchy, age, and gender prescription and the right to choose one's own culture. Difficult as it may be to discuss, define, measure, and even sometimes agree on the idea of cultural rights, without honoring, exploring, and respecting the cultural rights set forth in Article 27 of the UDHR and Article 15 of

---

[115] Rafael Capurro, "Information Ethics For and From Africa," *Journal of the American Society for Information Science and Technology* 59:7: 1167.

the ICESCR, African libraries will continue to reflect some part of the colonial past.

Given the traditions of social justice and human rights inherent in the core values of the Anglo-American tradition of librarianship discussed earlier in this chapter, and the principles set forth in the statutes of IFLA, our most international representation of the library profession, librarians and information workers in the global North who are engaged with African libraries at any level must take a closer look at the implications of cultural rights presented in our International Bill of Human Rights. Here I would argue that the language of ICESCR Article 15, recognizing the right of everyone to "take part in cultural life" is a more useful umbrella under which to stand in that it does not limit us to thinking that there is just one cultural community to serve. Most African communities, regardless of size, contain multiple ethnic, linguistic, gender, age-specific, socio-economic, and religious sub-communities. An individual within a particular sub-community may feel that a different sub-community is more relevant to his or her needs because of a change in religious or political identity or due to a change in socio-economic, marital, or educational status. These personal migrations of identity reveal the fluidity of cultural identity and must be respected by librarians and information workers seeking to meet the needs of all members of the community.

As revealed by the rhetoric of African librarians and information workers, and those from the global North who have also taken up their call, workers involved in building and supporting sustainable and responsive community-centered libraries in an African context must question all assumptions of Northern models of information provision imposed both during colonialism and now continued in the age of rapid globalization if they are to fully realize the cultural rights inherent in library work. There is a tendency in some quarters, both on and off the continent, to believe that the adoption of ICTs with their potential for digitizing local content and making audio and video formats more accessible, will do much to "level the playing field" in terms of flow of information from North to South while also expanding locally relevant materials and thus achieving a certain realization of cultural rights. This is a dangerous assumption, based once again on solutions from outside, and often not adequately taking into account the economic and power dynamics underlying ICT transfers. As both Raseroka and Capurro have pointed out, unless existing disparities and traditions which work against equity, access, and cultural rights are addressed, the use of ICTs will only amplify current conditions.

Without the recognition and respect of cultural rights, librarians and information workers engaged in African information provision, whether from within the continent or the global North, will be providing a roadblock for the full provision and realization of all human rights as stated in the UDHR. Human rights, as set forth and recognized in this document, are indivisible. We can not pick or choose our favorites. We cannot decide that it is our task as information workers to allow access to information but that we will keep that access only available in the languages of the colonial past. Similarly, we cannot decide that we will contribute to the right to access to education, but only if that education is based on the written word. Library and information workers engaged on the African continent must examine the needs of all communities and sub-communities within which they work, the existing cultural traditions of information provision already at play within those communities, and the economic realities that will determine sustainability. They must then base their library philosophy and services on those conditions rather than modeling them on an imposed notion or structure of information provision simply because it has become the internationally accepted "norm." Without such an approach, it is highly likely that we will be looking back fifty years from now and seeing the same problems wearing different technological garb.

# Cultural Rights and Language Rights in Libraries

Frans Albarillo

## Introduction

The purpose of this chapter is to examine cultural rights and language rights, and the contribution of these rights to our understanding of multiculturalism in libraries. The literature assembled here is largely interdisciplinary and draws from legal scholarship, political theory, linguistics, anthropology, and librarianship. I begin by providing some definitions of cultural rights and the way the concept of cultural rights emerges from Article 27 of the Universal Declaration of Human Rights (UDHR). I then discuss the important role of language in culture and the interconnectedness of cultural rights and language rights. I follow with a proposal that as librarians we must develop our philosophy of practice and consider the idea of language as a cultural right.

Considering language as a cultural right leads to the notion that equity of access to information can be framed as a universal right to information. By adopting the language of the UDHR as a framework, we can adopt concepts like cultural rights, found in Article 27, to give librarianship the vocabulary, analytical methods, and body of theory that strengthens our commitment to multilingual and multicultural societies in which universal access to information is viewed as a basic group and individual right. Historically, the library is the only social institution whose central mission is to provide access to information. By mapping and aligning our professional values of librarianship to reflect the fundamental assumption that a person's access to information is a basic universal right, we can begin to see the library as a vehicle for promoting language as a cultural right. Because the vast majority of information is transmitted via language, linguistic rights and cultural rights must be at the forefront of any argument for universal access to information. As the social, economic, and political forces of globalization and global migration transform public institutions worldwide, the social institution we know as the library is well positioned to lead innovative and critical dialogues about the role of language and information in our society.

## Defining Cultural Rights

There are several definitions of cultural rights. Fundamental to many of them is Article 27 of the UDHR, which states that "everyone has the right freely to participate in the cultural life of the community, to enjoy the arts and to share in scientific advancement and its benefits."[1] The exact meaning of this "ability freely to participate in cultural life" can be ambiguous, but if we consider an opposing idea of cultural persecution based on ethnicity, religion, or language, we can immediately appreciate the value of pluralism in societies. It was the shadow of Nazi Germany that caused the writers of the Declaration to explore the relationship between cultural and physical genocide.[2] Cultural rights are the rights of any person to practice his or her culture. It is important to understand that many features of cultural rights are fiercely debated. Aspects such as their implementation, their function in society, and their relationship with nation states continue to be negotiated at local, national, and international levels. Despite the difficulty in pinpointing clear definitions for cultural rights, we do know when they are violated, as exemplified in the genocides of this past century. Reactions to the destruction of cultural sites and other symbols of culture constantly reaffirm "the notion that a society should tolerate ethnic, racial, and religious diversity –pluralism-..."[3] The doctrine

---

[1] United Nations, "The Universal Declaration of Human Rights," http://www.un.org/en/documents/udhr/ (April 9, 2010).

[2] Johannes Morsink, "Cultural Genocide, the Universal Declaration, and Minority Rights," *Human Rights Quarterly* 21:4 (1999): 1009-1060.

[3] Robert L. Maddex, *International Encyclopedia of Human Rights: Freedoms, Abuses, and Remedies* (Washington, D.C.: CQ Press, 2000), 72.

of cultural rights is meant to protect cultural pluralism from the dangerous ideologies of cultural purity and should never be thought of as something than can be divorced from the historical context of genocide.

Cultural rights legal scholar Elsa Stamatopoulou defines five elements of cultural rights that derive from Article 27 of the UDHR and Article 15 of the International Covenant on Economic, Social and Cultural Rights and are recognized by international law:

1. the right to education;

2. the right to participate in cultural life;

3. the right to enjoy scientific progress and its applications;

4. the right to benefit from the protection of moral and material interests resulting from any scientific, literary or artistic production of which the person is the author, and

5. the freedom for scientific research and creative activity.[4]

The rights highlighted by Stamatopoulou emphasize the dynamics between the individual and the collective aspect of cultural rights. Cultural rights are the rights of both groups and individuals to freely practice and have access to their own forms of cultural expression, to preserve their distinct knowledge and their language, and to be able to transmit this knowledge inter- and intra-generationally. Implied in this definition are the rights to education, participation in culture life, scientific progress and its applications, and pursuing cultural heritage and forms of cultural expression.

Another important distinction that adds a layer to how we understand cultural rights is that cultural rights are seen as a third generation in the evolution of thinking about human rights. According to human rights historian Paul Gordon Lauren, first gen-

---

[4] Elsa Stamatopoulou, *Cultural Rights in International Law: Article 27 of the Universal Declaration of Human Rights and Beyond*, The Universal Declaration of Human Rights (Leiden; Boston: Martinus Nijhoff, 2007), 2-3.

eration civil and political rights were a product of the revolutions of the seventeenth and eighteenth centuries. Second generation economic and social rights resulted from the socialist and Marxist revolutions. Third generation collective rights came out of the anti-colonialist revolution following World War II and focused on self-determination, economic and social development, and environmental health.[5]

The implication for librarianship is that culture is a powerful factor when it comes to serving minority populations and defining multicultural librarianship. Culture, whether it is expressed in religion, ethnicity or spoken language, needs to be reflected in our collections, internet access, and professional training, with an emphasis on cultural differences as a celebration of diversity rather than a politics of difference and indifference.

### Article 27 and cultural rights

It is important that librarians recognize the issues surrounding a cultural rights approach. Though many controversies exist, there are two main problems in the debate over the legitimacy of cultural rights. The first problem is how to reconcile individual and collective rights when they come into conflict. The second is the classification of collectives or minority groups. Both problems are already familiar to librarians. For example, the broad themes found in conflicting individual and collective rights can also be seen in the debates concerning intellectual freedom and social responsibility.[6] Librarians also frequently struggle with the question of how to define different groups in the communities they are serving. Two vital sources in this discussion are Stamatopoulou's *Cultural Rights in International Law: Article 27 of the Universal Declaration of Human Rights*

---

[5] Paul Gordon Lauren, *The Evolution of International Human Rights: Visions Seen* 2nd ed., Pennsylvania Studies in Human Rights (Philadelphia: University of Pennsylvania Press, 2003), 295-296.

[6] John Swan et al., *The Freedom to Lie: A Debate About Democracy* (Jefferson, N.C.: McFarland, 1989).

*and Beyond* and Johannes Morsink's *The Universal Declaration of Human Rights, Origins, Drafting, and Intent.*[7] One recurring question in the debate over cultural rights is what to do when cultural rights conflict with individual rights. For example, "in some societies the practice of female genital mutilation . . . is a cultural tradition, but it is also widely condemned regardless of cultural status."[8] The problem of reconciling the rights of the individual with the rights of the group when they come into conflict is difficult to solve. In the literature this is often seen as the conflict between first generation individual rights and cultural rights, which are derived from individual rights and known as collective rights. In order to understand the problems of intellectual legitimacy surrounding cultural rights, this section attempts to sketch out Stamatopoulou's approach to what she calls "a cultural rights regime."[9] My main focus when reading her work is to understand its implications on the development of social institutions like libraries.

Stamatopoulou's response to the individual versus collectivity critique is that governments should follow a cultural policy that engages pluralistic democracy, emphasizing the nation state's need to recognize the multicultural realities of minorities and immigrants (collective rights) living in their borders. This recognition should ideally be positive with regards to the state and its social institutions, and individuals should retain their own individual rights. A mechanism for conflict mediation should be in place should conflict between individual and collective rights occur. In other words, there should be a system in place to mediate disputes on a case-by-case basis. In our example of traditional female genital mutilation, there should be an institution in society whose purpose is to deal with these types of sensitive cultural issues that arise from conflicts between individual and collective rights. Stamatopoulou is clearly

[7] Johannes Morsink, *The Universal Declaration of Human Rights: Origins, Drafting, and Intent*, Pennsylvania Studies in Human Rights (Philadelphia: University of Pennsylvania Press, 1999).

[8] Maddex, *International Encyclopedia of Human Rights*, 72.

[9] Stamatopoulou, *Cultural Rights in International Law*, 115-160.

thinking about a legal structure that will be sensitive to cultural issues of traditional societies as opposed to the absence of such an
institution or the existence of an institution that does not factor
culture into its decisions. Factoring culture into legal structures
cannot be done in broad strokes.

In the case of libraries, applying a cultural rights regime means
creating policies and structures that negotiate conflict between individuals and groups and looking critically at how we provide services to and define groups. Language is a good example because it is
an element of culture that librarians do not usually actively think
about, but it has great influence on the type of services they provide. Language is a major factor in selecting books, staffing, cataloging and classification, and ultimately access to information. Creating a structure for multilingual library services is just one aspect
of how a cultural rights regime can be applied to libraries. The
broader question here is how we can transform our libraries to realize and overcome cultural barriers to information access and dissemination. This will be explored further later in the chapter. In
addition to helping with the quandary of individual versus collective rights, Stamatopoulou's work is also helpful in characterizing
groups and their associated collective rights. It is crucial for librarians to understand her legal approach to the classification of peoples and groups as they are recognized by international law.

Who is a minority? Are migrants a minority? Are indigenous
people minorities? How do we provide services to Spanish speakers who are no longer a minority in many areas? And what about
the incredible diversity within that group of Spanish speakers?
These are some questions that plague the application of cultural
rights. Groups can call themselves whatever they want and practice
customs, speak their language, and disseminate their culture without the benefit of positive action by the state to support their
status. However, legal recognition of a group at a local, national, or
international level is probably the most empowering type of recognition because it affords the group visibility within a political system, a voice, and perhaps the ability to participate in the state's institutions. In the case of libraries this could mean federal funding

to establish an indigenous library or money to create cultural collections where they are appropriate. Collectives fall under what Stamatopoulou classifies as "special groups," based on international law, and include indigenous people and cultural minorities, religious groups, and migrant workers.[10] She also considers women, children and youth, persons with disabilities, and the poor as collectives.[11] Her application of a cultural rights regime to these collectives is inclusive of how social and economic effects create the need for monitoring and protecting cultural rights, since these rights are so closely entwined with the ultimate goal of creating cultural awareness of collectives and building intercultural tolerance within the state (through representation, resource allocation, and so on). Although there are many similarities between the legal and library terminology used to describe groups and collectives, the main difference in a human rights approach is really learning to look beyond the numbers. At the center of Article 27 and cultural rights is the value of pluralism. Avoiding any attempt to frame cultures as equal, but instead seeing each as different and celebrating that difference, is really a paradigm shift in the way we think. I think that this is a crucial step in building what Stamatopoulou calls a cultural rights regime in which social institutions like libraries help build tolerant, multicultural, multilingual societies.

In 1999, reflecting on the 50th anniversary of the UDHR, Morsink called the Declaration a success despite the flaws that have been identified in the UDHR. This single document has seeded many other declarations, covenants, and treaties[12] and has served as the foundational document for many NGOs and monitoring agencies. Lauren notes that "the Universal Declaration greatly assisted in the important process of setting standards, or establishing norms, for other declarations and legally binding conventions covering a wide variety of international human rights."[13] It is even

---

[10] Ibid., 163-200.

[11] Ibid., 230-44.

[12] Morsink, *The Universal Declaration of Human Rights*, ix-xiii.

[13] Lauren, *The Evolution of International Human Rights*, 234.

more exceptional to contemplate the influence of a single article - Article 27 - on the following documents: the 1966 International Covenant on Civil and Political Rights and the International Covenant on Economic, Social and Cultural Rights (ratified in force in 1976), the Limburg Principles on the Implementation of the International Covenant on Economic, Social and Cultural Rights (1986), the 1990 International Convention on the Protection of the Rights of All Migrant Workers and Members of Their Families (UN), the Declaration on the Rights of Persons Belonging to National or Ethnic, Religious and Linguistic Minorities (UN) 1992, the 1996 Barcelona Universal Declaration of Linguistic Rights (un-adopted), Masstricht Guidelines on Violations of Economic, Social and Cultural Rights (1997) UNESCO's 2001 Declaration on Cultural Diversity, and the Declaration on the Rights of Indigenous Peoples (2007). Some of these documents can be found in the appendices of Stamatopoulou,[14] and they establish the presence of cultural rights as an emerging body of law.

**Cultural rights and linguistic rights**

Information in the future will be multilingual, multi-format, and multi-cultural. Like information, librarianship is in the midst of transformation. It is now time to consider the role of language and cultural rights. Why language? The answer is simple - most information is mediated through language. The Internet and its associated technologies have opened the library to the world and drastically changed the nature of access to information. As libraries start using this technology to expand the audience they reach, we must learn to think as global citizens in order to remain relevant. Our patrons will look to us to find online newspapers, addresses of businesses, genealogical information, Skype accounts, foreign language fonts, marriage information, army service information, political conditions, and information on the wars in Afghanistan and Iraq. Another reason why librarians should move towards adopting an internationalist perspective has to do with the status of the United States as a global power. Our citizens are involved indirectly

---

[14] Stamatopoulou, *Cultural Rights in International Law*, 261-312.

or directly in international economic, military and social action. Socially responsible librarianship includes being able to connect users to information sources of different formats and languages so that our citizens have access to a variety of resources and remain informed. Providing access to a variety of information types will require language training and cultural diversification of the library workforce. There is already a movement in this direction with visible initiatives like Spectrum, an ALA scholarship program promoting diversity within librarianship. We also see the rise and the continued support of ethnic caucuses of the American Library Association. American libraries are on the road to diversification of library services and library staff to meet the growing needs of a clearly multicultural society. One of the main challenges that local libraries face is adapting to the changing multicultural landscape and immigration patterns of the communities they serve. Spoken and written language plays a key role in the creation, classification, and distribution of information. Language does not wholly encompass the totality of culture, but as a major aspect of culture it provides a unique insight into the social aspects of information. This leads to the question of whether language is a type of cultural right and to the broader question of how we can transform our libraries to realize and overcome cultural barriers to information access and dissemination.

Article 19 affirms the universal right to freedom of expression, and because language is a vehicle of expression it follows that language rights must be protected.[15] Freedom of speech is also supported in Article IV of the Library Bill of Rights, as explained in interpretation 2.18 in ALA's *Intellectual Freedom Manual*.[16] While neither of these last two documents specifically mentions language, it is definitely implied as an essential component of free expression. Susanna Mancini and Bruno De Witte establish linguistic rights as

---

[15] De Witte in Rainer Enrique Hamel, "Introduction: Linguistic Human Rights in a Sociolinguistic Perspective," *International Journal of the Sociology of Language* 127 (1997): 5.

[16] American Library Association, *Intellectual Freedom Manual* (Chicago: American Library Association, 2006), 206-209.

grounded in Article 19, taking the following position on protecting the linguistic component of freedom of expression: "Although most constitutional and international fundamental rights documents protect freedom without highlighting the linguistic component of this freedom, that component is inherently a part of freedom of expression. The same is true with equality and non-discrimination."[17] From this point of view, language rights can be considered an individual right. However, language can also, as a defining characteristic of a cultural group, be considered a collective right.

Stamatopoulou refers to language rights as "hidden rights" that are implied by the wording of Article 27.[18] Inferring language rights from Article 27 means that free participation in the cultural life of a community must also include the right to languages spoken in minority communities. As I have argued above, it can be shown that language as a component of the freedom of expression can be viewed as an individual right, but it is also a collective right because language is a salient feature of a cultural group. A conservative interpretation, according to Morsink, means that language cannot be claimed as part of Article 27.[19] However, the interrelatedness of individual rights moving from the civil/political to the social/economic/collective seems to imply the conditions for basic universal human rights cannot be met if certain economic, social, and collective rights are not guaranteed. For example, this logic can be seen in how the 1966 International Covenant on Civil and Political Rights did mention language and added to its own Article 27 a provision for the rights of "persons belonging to ethnic, linguistic or religious minorities to enjoy their own culture."[20] Article 27 of

---

[17] Susanna Mancini and Bruno de Witte, "Culture, Heritage, and Human Rights: An Introduction," in *Cultural Human Rights* ed. Francesco Francioni and Martin Scheinin, *International Studies in Human Rights* (Leiden; Boston: Martinus Nijhoff Publishers, 2008), 249.

[18] *Stamatoupolou, Cultural Rights in International Law*, 107.

[19] Morsink, *The Universal Declaration of Human Rights*, 269.

[20] Francesco Francioni, "Culture, Heritage, and Human Rights: An Introduction," in *Cultural Human Rights* ed. Francesco Francioni and

the International Covenant on Civil and Political Rights points to
language rights as a collective right with the explicit intention of
protecting minorities' freedom to enjoy their own culture. The
logic here is that basic human rights, including freedom of speech,
cannot be protected without ensuring the economic and social vi-
ability of collective groups. Although minorities were never a part
of the original wording of the UDHR, subsequent declarations and
conventions have articulated the minority position. Notable examples are the Declaration on the Rights of Persons Belonging to National or Ethnic, Religious and Linguistic Minorities and the Declaration on the Rights of Indigenous Peoples.

The organic unity of the UDHR means that all the articles are
meant to be read as a whole. According to Morsink "the drafters
wanted the readers of the Declaration to interpret each article in
light of all others. Most of them believed that the exact place of an
article was not crucial to its meaning since it needed to be interpreted in the context of the whole anyway."[21] This organic character of the text applies to how it grew to be what it is now, as well as
to a deeper interconnectedness of all the articles. During the World
Conference on Human Rights in 1993, delegates declared that civil,
political, economic, social, and cultural rights are indivisible, interdependent and interrelated.[22] Following this organic approach it is
clear that linguistic rights are supported in the interrelatedness of
Articles 19 and 27.

There is considerable literature about language, minorities, and
human rights, and scholars writing on these issues include linguists
who look at the role of language policy on speakers of minority
languages. Tove Skutnabb-Kangas and Robert Phillipson's *Linguistic Human Rights: Overcoming Linguistic Discrimination* is a collection of
edited papers that make a case for mother-tongue education as

---

Martin Scheinin, *International Studies in Human Rights* (Leiden: Martinus
Nijhoff Publishers, 2008), 9.

[21] Morsink, *The Universal Declaration of Human Rights*, 232.

[22] Stamatopoulou, *Cultural Rights in International Law*, 19.

fundamental to minority language speakers.[23] Fernand de Varennes's *Language, Minorities and Human Rights* is a comprehensive
analysis of legal cases that involve language and the state and shows
how decisions made in the legal system relating to language contribute to the negative perception and continued marginalization of
minority cultures and the languages they speak.[24] Stephen May's
*Language and Minority Rights: Ethnicity, Nationalism and the Politics of
Language*, first published in 2001 and reprinted in 2008, explores the
history and evolution of the minority language rights issue and focuses on the political aspects of language policy.[25]

As libraries work to promote cultural rights through an understanding of Article 27, they must think carefully about both the
individual and collective aspects of language access in information
work. This means incorporating as part of the librarian's information repertoire new media, new formats, and new resources in languages that previously were not on the information radar. For example, in an article by journalist David Lee called "Wikipedia's Future in Africa" Jimmy Wales, the founder of Wikipedia, stated: "We
have a very strong view that access to information is a fundamental
human right. We're about trying to provide that neutral voice." The
short article continues to talk about the lack of presence of other
languages online and how this linguistic deficit needs to be reme-
died if access to information is indeed treated as a fundamental
human right. According to Wales, Wikipedia was banned in China
for three years, and to this day certain topics like Taiwan continue
to be filtered by the government; however, this has not deterred
Wikipedia's expansion to non-English speaking areas.[26]

Why should librarians care about language and cultural rights?
There is a power relationship between information, language, and

---

[23] Tove Skutnabb-Kangas and Robert Phillipson, eds., *Linguistic Human
Rights: Overcoming Linguistic Discrimination* (Berlin: Walter de Gruyter,1995).
[24] Fernand de Varennes, *Language, Minorities and Human Rights*,
International Studies in Human Rights (The Hague: M. Nijhoff, 1996).
[25] Stephen May, *Language and Minority Rights: Ethnicity, Nationalism and the
Politics of Language* (New York: Routledge, 2008).
[26] Dave Lee, "Wikipedia's Future in Africa," *BBC World Service* 2009.

culture. Consider why it is that only developed countries that speak a global language like English are the main beneficiaries of technologies that allow access to information. This omnipresence of English information could arguably be a new hegemony. As librarians we understand the limited view of Dewey's classification system, or LC subject headings as applied to non-western concepts; English-based ontologies make access and the search for information difficult for those who do not use this *lingua franca*. A cultural rights approach recognizes that the lack of linguistic diversity has already led to an imbalanced information presence. So it is a positive sign that Wikipedia has 10,000 entries in Swahili.[27] If knowledge is power then we need to think about how certain types of knowledge are mediated through language. The presence or nonpresence of other modes of linguistic communication in the way we structure our information has serious implications for library collections as they are reinvented in their digital form. Librarians and libraries involved in digital initiatives are currently setting the future of practice. There is an ethical issue here that needs to be explored between the practice of knowledge organizations like libraries and how best to approach information, language, and culture as we develop new models of scholarship, publishing, access, and best practices in managing collections, whether they are virtual collections or physical. Language rights are not just an issue of access, but should be thought of as central to the other types of knowledge as represented in culture.

Wikipedia is but one of the new forms of information that has tremendous potential in developing countries. We are exploring educational approaches to mobile technologies - Twitter in Iran and Haiti, and blogging in the Middle East. In the United States, public libraries are changing in many ways. Queens Public Library has a website in six different languages and boasts an International Resource Center that has material in 59 different languages.[28] In Portland, Oregon, Multnomah County Library's *Target Language*

---

[27] Ibid.

[28] Queens Borough Public Library, "Queens Library," http://www.queenslibrary.org/ (April 9, 2010).

*Initiative* aims at "increasing bilingual staffing, improving training for all library staff (particularly those in locations that serve immigrant communities)," and "growing the library's collection and expanding programming."[29] It is clear that these two libraries serve exceptionally diverse communities where there is a need and support for such activities. These trends in the linguistic and cultural diversification of our urban centers will only continue. Facilitating pluralism means taking language, information, and power seriously.

## Developing our philosophy of practice

Not only do many developing countries struggle economically, but there also are many social struggles that have created the need for cultural rights. Will Kymlicka and Alan Patten[30] point to the growing body of legal work on political theory that focuses on language as a flashpoint for cultural conflict. UNESCO Director General Koichiro Matsuura expressed the importance of intercultural dialogue in the shadow of September 11, 2001 in his introduction to the Declaration on Cultural Diversity. He praises the UDHR, "which makes it clear that each individual must acknowledge otherness in its own forms but also the plurality of his or her own identity, within societies that are themselves plural."[31] This celebration of diversity and promotion of cultural pluralism should be a part of our vision of the future library and of librarianship. The library must be viewed as a social institution that provides spaces in society where inter- and intra-cultural dialogue can take place. This idea of cultivating inter- and intra-group social capital can be found in the work of political theorist Robert Putnam.[32] By embracing cultural rights and cultural pluralism, libraries can play a crucial role

---

[29] Multnomah County Library, "Multnomah County Library," http://www.multcolib.org/ (April 9, 2010).
[30] Will Kymlicka and Alan Patten, *Language Rights and Political Theory* (Oxford: Oxford University Press, 2003), 1-52.
[31] Koichiro Matsuura, "Introduction," in *Unesco Universal Declaration on Cultural Diversity*, ed. 31st Session of the General Conference of UNESCO (Paris: 2001).
[32] Robert D. Putnam, Lewis M. Feldstein, and Don Cohen, *Better Together: Restoring the American Community* (New York: Simon & Schuster, 2004).

in building tolerant multicultural societies as they provide physical and virtual spaces that can serve as a public forum for cultural dialogue, debate and discovery.

A philosophy of librarianship that includes language as a cultural right aligns itself with the present reality of the communities we serve and moves away from our past history of an English-centered library practice. I stated in the introduction that one of the core missions of libraries, as social institutions, has been to provide access to information. I believe this remains true today; many of our social critiques of libraries revolve around the question of who has the right to access and use the library. Acknowledging language as a cultural right is the first step to what I believe can be a powerful way to reframe the idea of access to information. Language is so "under the hood" with regards to our daily consumption of information that we do not usually question its implications for access and information. As publishing technologies proliferate and media and information converge, it is clear that in the future the distribution of information will no longer be a physical challenge, but rather a social one. Librarians need to explore the opportunities here for libraries as social institutions that work to secure these cultural rights for their communities by facilitating access of information with the goal of creating informed citizenry. Library services to immigrants and minorities have become a centerpiece of the American Library Association's commitment to multiculturalism. *Rocks in the Whirlpool*[33] and *Equity of Access*[34] are works that show how librarians have been committed to providing equitable access to library services in diverse communities, both historically and at present. "Equity of access" is the primary metaphor that our profession uses to discuss questions about the value of serving diverse communities, but is this metaphor adequate enough to deal with

---

[33] Kathleen de la Peña McCook, "Rocks in the Whirlpool," American Library Association, http://www.ala.org/ala/aboutala/missionhistory/keyactionareas/equityaction/rockswhirlpool.cfm (April 9, 2010).

[34] American Library Association, *Equity of Access* (Chicago: American Library Association, 2004).

the complexities of equity and access in the context of today's information societies?

Social, economic, technological, and political forces are transforming our industrial societies to information societies. The world is interconnected. People are communicating, exchanging information, and sharing ideas more rapidly than at any other time in history. Equity of access acknowledges the need for access to information as fundamental to immigrants or minorities.[35] However, this philosophy is incomplete in that it does not do enough to facilitate intercultural tolerance and is, in fact, silent on cultural rights.

The metaphor "equity of access" continues to draw the minority and majority distinction, where minorities are relatively subordinate to majority cultures. It is essential to recognize cultural minorities living within a larger culturally homogenous state in relation to universal human rights. Cultural recognition is just a composite piece of the social, economic, and political elements that make up the goal of allowing life with dignity. Our present framework of "equity of access" recognizes minorities in the context of the state. The distinction in this framework is that minority culture is not majority culture and the importance of culture with regards to minorities is something determined by the state rather than something that is universal. Services are allocated with a "by the numbers" approach. For example, a library might adjust its collection, staffing, and hours according to the demographics of the community it serves. It might allocate five percent of its collection budget because five percent of a population belongs to a demographic ethnic group that speaks a different language. Is providing this equitable access the same thing as supporting the right of everyone "freely to participate in the cultural life of the community, to enjoy the arts and to share in scientific advancement and its benefits"? By framing the question in these terms we see that a "by the numbers" approach falls short of understanding the distinctiveness of implementing cultural rights in practice.

---

[35] Katherine J. Phenix and Kathleen de la Peña McCook, "Human Rights and Librarians," Reference & User Services Quarterly 45:1 (2005): 23-26.

Librarians must do more than open the door to information. The profession must completely rethink the role of culture and information. Language is a central aspect of the cultural dimension of information. Librarians must go beyond equal access and ask themselves if there is value in recognizing that information and knowledge are culturally produced. If knowledge and information are indeed the product of culture then what is the role of language in facilitating the enjoyment of the arts? How does language allow sharing in scientific advancement, and what structures can libraries put in place so that many people can benefit from the common effort of all cultures that produce knowledge about the human condition? A re-imagining of the role of the library in society is necessary to ensure relevance as library services and cooperation grow beyond its walls to work locally, nationally, and internationally.

**The Universal Declaration of Human Rights as a framework**

"These freedoms of expression and worship—of access to information and political participation – we believe are universal rights. They should be available to all people, including ethnic and religious minorities – whether they are in the United States, China, or any nation."[36]

Is President Obama correct in saying that access to information is a universal right and that nation states should take action to ensure that this right is available to all people, including ethnic and religious minorities? How does a statement like this affect the contemporary field of librarianship? Librarians should start with the UDHR. The UDHR, and especially Article 27, will give librarians a general framework and vocabulary for approaching the issue of multiculturalism and librarianship. Is access to information a universal right? Can it be articulated and supported within our profession? I believe that the universal right to access information can be enriched by critical discussions on language and cultural rights by

---

[36] Barack Obama, "Remarks by President Barack Obama at Town Hall Meeting with Future Chinese Leaders," (2009).

looking at how language can be either a barrier or facilitator to information.

Adopting a human rights approach to librarianship means understanding what would compel a body of statesmen and stateswomen, philosophers, diplomats, and legal experts to believe that certain rights, among them Article 27's right freely to participate in the cultural life of the community, to enjoy the arts, and to share in scientific advancement and its benefits, are universal. The intent behind Article 27, which was written over 60 years ago, is still debated today. However, if our philosophy of librarianship includes a deep commitment to advancing equity and fostering pluralism in our democracy, an examination is needed to give weight to why multicultural and multilingual library services are so fundamental in securing the value of a human being's right to information in society.

**Mapping professional values**

When examining the UDHR, librarians should recognize the themes of intellectual freedom and social responsibility, censorship, and access to information. Librarians have a long tradition of engaging with these values. Professional training for librarians includes an introduction to policy documents like the *Intellectual Freedom Manual*.[37] I have noticed that our profession has shown alignment to Article 19 of the UDHR in particular, citing it to strengthen the cause of intellectual freedom. The value of diversity as expressed in ALA's Policy Manual (Section 60) could also be used to support Article 27 and cultural rights:

> The American Library Association (ALA) promotes equal access to information for all persons and recognizes the ongoing need to increase awareness of and responsiveness to the diversity of the communities we serve. ALA recognizes the critical need for access to library and information resources, services, and technologies by all people, especially those who may experience language or literacy-related barriers. ... Libraries can and should

---

[37] American Library Association, *Intellectual Freedom Manual*. (Chicago: American Library Association, 2006).

play a crucial role in empowering diverse populations for full participation in a democratic society.[38]

Earlier versions of this policy were not as explicit in including language as a barrier to information. What is interesting about this latest revision of the ALA Policy Manual is that it connects language and culture to "full participation in a democratic society" and emphasizes how libraries can provide access to information for any citizen or immigrant to help him or her have a voice in a deliberative democracy.

Before we leap without looking, part of the purpose in advocating a stance in support of UDHR and Article 27 in this chapter is to encourage librarians to create their own discourses and examine the language that surrounds the UDHR in the context of librarianship. As critical readers and thinkers, librarians must ask themselves whether human and cultural rights are really universal across all cultures. Do we need to enter this complicated argument and find our own uses for terms like cultural relativism, international relations, and genocide? Scholar Toni Samek believes that human rights and librarianship have a close relationship:

> How can opportunities provided by information and communications technologies, interconnectivity and the global digital network be applied to ameliorate discriminatory knowledge practices to make them accessible to all? To what extent can improved library and information practices redress the failed promotion of cultural distinctiveness, cultural literacy, cultural democracy and democratic education? How can people working in the information and communication technologies fields (and sharing the principle that knowledge and information access is free, open and egalitarian for everybody) consciously improve knowledge practices to facilitate the democratization of informa-

---

[38] American Library Association, "ALA Policy Manual," http://www.ala.org/ala/aboutala/governance/policymanual/index.cfm (April 9, 2010).

tion and knowledge and the prerequisite promotion and cultural diversity?[39]

Understanding global information and taking an internationalist approach means being comfortable with the fluidity of information and information technologies. In *Librarianship and Human Rights: A Twenty-First Century Guide,* Samek frames her arguments with the idea of librarians being able to affect social change.[40] It is clear that one of the places of information convergence is the library, and her book suggests that the library is especially situated in society to become an institution that can provide access for people who otherwise would not enjoy the benefits of the information society. This social responsibility is a hallmark of Samek's work. The socially responsible librarian provides his or her community with information to become empowered, and uses it to fight discrimination, racism, and propaganda.

Mapping human and cultural rights to our basic duties as librarians means building cultural collections, providing culturally appropriate means of organization so that information is accessible, and making sure that these resources are optimal for the community we serve. It means increased cultural programming in other languages, and cross-cultural and language training for staff. These recommendations are not new and can be found in the literature of library services and outreach to minority populations. For example, library scholar Cheryl Metoyer-Duran reviews public library and information science literature from 1985 to 1991 and analyzes how public libraries have responded by creating programs to target speakers of minority languages.[41] Sondra Cuban's chapter on building collections for new immigrant communities synthesizes best practices and resources for multilingual and multicultural collec-

---

[39] Toni Samek, *Librarianship and Human Rights: A Twenty-First Century Guide,* Chandos Information Professional Series (Oxford: Chandos, 2007), 15.

[40] Ibid., 15.

[41] Cheryl Metoyer-Duran, *Gatekeepers in Ethnolinguistic Communities,* Information Management, Policy, and Services (Norwood, NJ: Ablex Pub. Corp., 1993).

tions[42] and also provides strategies for reducing barriers to collection use and for overcoming cost barriers.[43] *Library Services to Indigenous Populations* explores history and issues specifically dealing with indigenous groups.[44] Other models of multilingual and multicultural librarianship are described by Adriana Tandler.[45] Patricia Overall proposes a cultural framework for LIS professionals in three areas: cognitive, interpersonal, and environmental.[46] She emphasizes the connections between culture and the construction of knowledge. Most importantly, she calls for the codification of cultural competencies in librarianship.[47] Information comes in many forms, ranging from the illuminated manuscript to the poems of Homer to a traditional Hawaiian mele. The form in which information takes place will also reflect the culture that produces it.

**Role of the library in promoting language and cultural rights**

Looking to Article 27 of the UDHR and adopting a human rights approach to culture will reshape our definitions of multicultural library services and will require a reframing of our present discussion of the many ways in which information, information technologies, and power have now largely been organized at the global level. A human rights approach to librarianship will ask questions that identify all of humanity as the community the library

---

[42] Sondra Cuban, *Serving New Immigrant Communities in the Library* (Westport, CT: Libraries Unlimited, 2007), 143-72.

[43] Ibid., 148-50.

[44] Kelly Webster, ed. *Library Services to Indigenous Populations: Viewpoints & Resources* (Chicago: Office for Literacy and Outreach Services, American Library Association, 2005), 32-62.

[45] Adriana Acauan Tandler, "New Americans Program: Outreach through Partnerships," in *From Outreach to Equity: Innovative Models of Library Policy and Practice*, ed. Robin Osborne and American Library Association. Office for Literacy and Outreach Services (Chicago: American Library Association, 2004).

[46] Patricia Montiel Overall, "Cultural Competence: A Conceptual Framework for Library and Information Science Professionals," *Library Quarterly* 79:2 (2009): 175.

[47] Ibid., 199.

is serving. This approach will not only consider how information access affects African Americans, but will also look to Africa and ask why are there large disparities of access to, for example, scientific research in Africa. Why can't we develop resource sharing at a global level? Although broader access to knowledge will not instantly, or completely, for that matter, solve problems of developing nations, librarians should be aware of the effects of disparities in information access technology between different countries. These disparities affect education at all levels. Librarianship that is focused on human rights will ask how we can influence our practices here to open our institutional repositories, health research, and digital library projects so that all may benefit. These questions are all concerned with how information and information structures are affecting human beings. Are we becoming human rights and cultural rights activists when we inquire whether a particular book or journal is available in a specific format or language? Librarians and libraries that are participating in open access and open source development are bringing into focus a human rights issue: access to information should be universal. The language that is used to convey information and to create libraries and universities will naturally give an advantage to the speakers of that language group. Today that language is largely English and it is accepted that English speakers have the advantage over non-English speakers.

> One may well ask what need librarians have to discuss issues of language and ethnic identity. However, in the best interests of those we serve – as well as the unserved and underserved – we must ask these questions. Do the materials we select for our collections provide a true and sensitive portrayal of the 'other Americans' ... Do we provide equitable access to informational materials and leisure reading by purchasing at least some items in the language of choice of one of seven residents in the United States? Have we adequately trained staff to be aware of subtle differences in social interactions among the different populations we serve?[48]

---

[48] Sonia Ramirez Wohlmuth, "Language and Identity in Contemporary Latin American Thought" (paper presented at the The power of language

So much of ethnicity and culture involves language, which arguably shapes our understanding of the world around us. Librarians must reshape the social institution of the library with a critical approach to language, culture, and information. We must be wary of a flattened social transcript where information structures exist only to service the majority of a population in a society. If we continue assuming that everyone speaks English, we are doing a disservice to the minorities and to the cultures and languages they have the right to practice in order to freely enjoy cultural life. Again, supporting language as a cultural right means looking beyond a "by the numbers" approach and beginning to envision a library that promotes action and egalitarianism.

In researching the "library as a social institution" two books heavily influenced the use of the term "library" in this chapter. These were John Budd's *Self-examination: The Present and Future of Librarianship*[49] and Charles Osburn's *The Social Transcript: Uncovering Library Philosophy*.[50] Budd locates the library as a core social institution in which citizens can access information as a primary function of a library in a democracy. He devotes an entire chapter to the exploration of the libraries, political philosophy, and governance, and takes the reader on a tour of democratic theory while pondering the role of the library as a social institution that actively communicates "the record – texts, images, sounds."[51] Budd describes the role of a library in a democracy as an "agent of the state" that should positively promote egalitarianism and the empowerment of groups.[52] This vision of librarianship is very much aligned with supporting a human rights approach to culture and cultural rights.

---

= El poder de la palabra: selected papers from the Second REFORMA National Conference, Englewood, CO, 2001), 4.

[49] John M. Budd, *Self-Examination: The Present and Future of Librarianship* (Westport, CT: Libraries Unlimited, 2008).

[50] Charles B. Osburn, *The Social Transcript: Uncovering Library Philosophy* (Westport, CT: Libraries Unlimited, 2009).

[51] Budd, *Self-Examination*, 182.

[52] Ibid., 183.

The value of egalitarianism can also be translated as a value that has transcended the "by the numbers" approach that I critiqued earlier by focusing on the equality of all groups. Empowering groups by treating them equally in terms of access to information facilitates civil discourse. However, I would like to draw a distinction between civil discourse and informed civil discourse.

Civil discourse can or cannot be "informed" depending on the particular citizen's or group's access to information resources and on whether these resources are culturally accessible. This claim includes ethnic considerations in terms of language acting as a barrier to information, or whether the language of information is comprehensible to the person who is requesting the information. The distinction here is about matching information needs with appropriate information resources. Informed civil discourse then requires not only working to increase the information literacy of a user, but also requires us to develop cultural dimensions of information literacy with respect to language. Imagine the various considerations in assisting a Latino user who may need Spanish language resources and a native speaker of English, both of whom are small business owners researching how best to file their taxes. The distinction then between informed civil discourse and civil discourse requires the pairing of culturally appropriate information in a language that user understands. The library as a social institution must evolve its definitions of culture as it relates to civil discourse and draw more precise distinctions when it comes to information needs of users, because in any political system the library is the only social intuition that serves as a resource for information.

Like Budd, Osburn is also concerned about "the record," but he argues that libraries are stewards of what he calls "the social transcript."[53] One criticism I have of Osburn's arguments is his heavy emphasis on the dominance of print cultures. Indeed, relatively little attention has been given to oral cultures. The nature of information today clearly shows that as technologies evolve we will face a new type of cultural record, and it will not be a static collection of print material with a model of publishing that we have in-

---

[53] Osburn, The Social Transcript.

herited since the invention of the printing press. The library as it relates to the social transcript or the cultural record will have to adjust to the dynamic stream of information coming from all over the world, in many languages, and from many points of view. The very nature of information (previously communicated through print material) is no longer limited to a physical format, which has led many people to believe that the library is no longer relevant. The library as a social institution has evolved to provide access to dynamic (electronic) and static (print) information while it continues to serve its more traditional functions of organizing, creating and disseminating resources in its own community. Again, we see the potential for the local, national, and global role of the library. As I stated earlier, barriers to information today are no longer physical, but are fundamentally social. In order to see past our local and national roles and imagine our relevance in a global culture where everyone is a minority, librarianship needs an international philosophical framework to connect our local and national practices to the international community of librarians.

**Conclusion**

In the first two sections I looked at what cultural rights are and at some theoretical issues in realizing Article 27 in a cultural rights regime. I drew heavily from the work of Stamatopoulou to outline the problems surrounding how a cultural rights regime might set up institutions and policies meant to systematically resolve conflicts that arise between individual human rights and cultural rights. In order to explore the idea that libraries should support a cultural rights regime I presented Stamatopoulou's legal research on how collectives and minority groups are classified in the framework of international law and suggested that librarians think critically about the categories we have created for collectives and minority groups. Rethinking our categories for collectives or groups is the first step to a critical approach in implementing a cultural rights regime in the library.

I followed with a discussion on language and how thinking critically about language and cultural rights will help us come closer to implementing a cultural rights approach to thinking about cul-

ture and group membership. I then argued that a human and cultural rights approach requires a fundamental shift from "equitable
access" and "by the numbers" policies to a broader understanding
that people have a universal right to information. This right to information is not just about access, but it is also about information
being cultural, produced and transmitted in a variety of ways as
represented in language, poetry, technology, and so on. In the following section I reviewed some of the literature on multicultural
librarianship and outreach to minority groups. In order to promote
language as a cultural right I covered John Budd's idea of egalitarianism and group empowerment and related it to Osburn's social
transcript, warning that the cultural record represented in our collections needs to be more balanced. For both authors, language and
communication are fundamental to their view of library work and I
believe that, because these elements are so fundamental, as a profession we should explore what Article 27 and cultural rights means
to our practice.

Cultural rights and language rights are fundamental to the social, economic, and political development and wellbeing of collectives. These rights must be protected, expanded and integrated into
the discussions of libraries and librarianship as a profession. Librarians and libraries will play a crucial role in fostering inter- and
intra-cultural tolerance and in doing so might be able to undo what
Nigerian writer Ngũgĩ wa Thiong'o calls the "cultural bomb":

> The biggest weapon wielded and actually daily unleashed by im-
> perialism against collective defiance is the cultural bomb. The ef-
> fect of a cultural bomb is to annihilate a people's belief in their
> names, in their language, in their environment, in their heritage
> of struggle, in their unity, in their capacities, and ultimately in
> themselves.[54]

Adopting a human rights approach in support of cultural rights and
language rights requires us to undo the effects of this cultural
bomb. It was during the postcolonial period following the writing

---

[54] Thiong'o Ngũgĩ wa, *Decolonising the Mind: The Politics of Language in
African Literature* (London: J. Currey, 1986), 3.

of the UDHR that social, economic, and collective rights evolved because these rights were necessary additions to ensure a standard of dignity for all peoples. The most powerful tool that librarians have is the ability to give people access to the knowledge our collections provide. A human rights approach acknowledges that all cultures are valuable and all cultures produce, often in their own languages, knowledge that contributes to our understanding of humanity. Our collections need to restore people's beliefs in their names, in their language, in their environment, in their heritage of struggle, in their unity, in their capacity, and ultimately in themselves. Access to information is fundamental in creating thriving, informed discussions and healthy democracies.

# We Collect, Organize, Preserve, and Provide Access, With Respect: Indigenous Peoples' Cultural Life in Libraries

## Loriene Roy and Kristen Hogan

There is no doubt that the text and sentiments behind Article 19 of the Universal Declaration of Human Rights (UDHR) resonate within the field of librarianship. Librarians support an individual's intellectual freedom to have access to a wide variety of information, and to hold opinions and to express them. Article 27 expands these rights to honor the individual ability to participate in the cultural life of the community and to have one's own creations, including writings, scientific pursuits, and artistic expressions, protected. These sentiments are centered on individual rights and, as such, these beliefs are not in agreement with an indigenous worldview, which places community rights above those of the individual and protects communal ownership of cultural expressions across generations. Does this explain why library workers might balk at the notion of protecting the knowledge representation of a group, especially that of an indigenous community? How do we begin to understand these differing viewpoints? How can such seemingly opposing beliefs result in individuals, professional organizations, and communities that are supportive and respectful of each other?

Attention to indigenous librarianship and indigenous human rights calls librarians, and others, to read the UDHR in its own cultural context. Doing so reveals that Article 19 cannot be fulfilled without Article 27 and its sister international documents on collective cultural rights. In order to support the "freedom of opinion and expression" of Article 19, librarians cannot remain neutral but must take collective responsibility to intervene in systems of oppression by advocating for and supporting the cultural self-determination of marginalized cultures, including indigenous cultures.

Since the UDHR is perhaps the most visible of human rights documents, we begin this article with a brief contextualization of Article 27. While cultural rights are often discussed as group rights, Article 27 confers rights on individuals. Elsa Stamatopoulou, Chief of the United Nations Forum on Indigenous Issues, explains that "Article 27 does not present a commitment to the respect of diversity and pluralism, since it assumes somehow that cultural participation will take place in the 'one' culture of the 'nation-state.'" During UDHR drafting in 1948, the U.S. and others opposed UDHR language protecting minorities; this opposition resulted in the exclusion of such protections.[1] Instead, Article 27's deceivingly universal language, "Everyone has the right freely to participate in *the* cultural life of *the* community," has produced poor support for cultural rights. Stamatopoulou suggests that "governments may be wary of the threat majorities may feel from the promotion of minority cultures which may lead to claims for collective rights."[2]

Reading Article 27 as part of a constellation of cultural rights documents emphasizes the cultural specificity of Article 27 itself. Rodolfo Stavenhagen, Mexican sociologist and UN Special Rapporteur on the Human Rights and Fundamental Freedoms of Indigenous Peoples, points out that the UDHR "does not mention minorities or any other human group, except the family."[3] This

---

[1] Elsa Stamatopoulou, "Why Cultural Rights Now?" Carnegie Council, September 23, 2004, http://www.cceia.org/resources/transcripts/5006.html (accessed 9 November 2009).

[2] Ibid.

[3] Rodolfo Stavenhagen, "Cultural Rights: A Social Science Perspective," in *Economic, Social and Cultural Rights: A Textbook*, eds. Abjørn Eide, Catarina Krause, Allan Rosas (Dordrecht, The Netherlands: Martinus Nijhoff Publishers, 2001), 85-110, 99.

choice undermined the universality of the document. During the 1948 drafting of the UDHR, Stavenhagen recounts, the American Anthropological Association submitted a statement to the UN Commission on Human Rights: "the universal declaration should not, said the American anthropologists, be conceived only in terms of the values prevalent in Western Europe and America."[4] Linda Tuhiwai-Smith, education scholar and Pro Vice-Chancellor Māori at the University of Waikato, explains, "The individual, as the basic social unit from which other social organizations and social relations form, is another system of ideas which needs to be understood as part of the West's cultural archive";[5] that is, Tuhiwai-Smith supports Stamatopoulou's interpretation that Article 27's support for the individual's right to participate in *the* cultural life of a national community is grounded in western values. Stavenhagen points out that this means that "[h]uman rights policies are not entirely neutral," and "the evolution of human rights thinking in different contexts should be seen as an ongoing process—a dialogic process."[6] Australian and U.S. humanities scholars Kay Schaffer and Sidonie Smith anticipated in 2004 that passage of the Declaration on the Rights of Indigenous Peoples would "significantly alter the parameters of rights discourse" by supporting "group rather than individual rights, encompassing the aspirations of indigenous and minority peoples for self-determination and their claims to culture, language, religion, and land rights, sometimes in opposition to states' claims of sovereignty."[7] After more than a decade of deliberation, the UN officially adopted the Declaration on the Rights of Indigenous Peoples in September of 2007, despite Australia, Canada, New Zealand, and the U.S. voting against its passage. As Kathleen de la Peña McCook and Katharine Phenix point out, "human rights values permeate library policies," thus bringing the daily work of librarians within the dialogue about hu-

---

[4] Ibid., 94.

[5] Linda Tuhiwai-Smith, *Decolonizing Methodologies: Research and Indigenous Peoples* (London: Zed Books, 1999), 49.

[6] Stavenhagen, "Cultural Rights," 99.

[7] Kay Schaffer and Sidonie Smith, *Human Rights and Narrated Lives: The Ethics of Recognition* (New York: Palgrave/MacMillan, 2004), 16.

man rights.[8] Librarians need to understand the history of human rights language and its meanings for indigenous communities in order to more fully enter these discussions.

We draw on this context for Article 27 as a foundation to use indigenous readings of culture to reframe interpretations of human rights and library practice. This chapter will take the familiar setting of libraries and their individual user-centered orientation and hold it next to the concept of indigenous worldview. Our reference points are indigenous expressions, historical events and U.S. policy over time, and key documents approved by and actions of the American Library Association (ALA) and other bodies. In order to demonstrate the urgency for librarians' attention to indigenous librarianship, we begin the chapter with an exploration of indigenous identity and the parallel histories of libraries and U.S. policy and their implications for indigenous peoples. Building on these histories, we turn to indigenous librarianship to inform definitions of culture and community in an interpretation of Article 27's first paragraph. We close our chapter with a look at what protecting moral and material interests, the substance of Article 27's second paragraph, means in an indigenous context for culture, and we offer suggestions for library practice. Thus said, we believe that in consciously engaging with Article 27 librarians can begin a consideration of the intersection between indigenous rights, their cultural expressions, and the service and philosophical missions of libraries.

**Who Are Indigenous Peoples?**

While library and information workers are educated to reach out to underserved populations, many in our field may be unfamiliar with even local Native patrons and groups. The fact that there are over 500 federally recognized tribes within the geographic borders of the United States, as well as over 100 non-federally recognized tribes, is not well known. In speaking about indigenous peoples, then, it may help to first consider who these people are, and especially how they would describe themselves. The connection

---

[8]Katharine J. Phenix and Kathleen de la Peña McCook, "Human Rights and Librarians," *Reference & User Services Quarterly* 45 (1) (Fall 2005): 23-26.

between naming and self-determination also has clear implications for indigenous library advocacy.

There are many definitions for indigenous. The editors of *Varua Tupu: New Writing from French Polynesia* explain that "this emphasis on names and naming is not trivial."[9] Naming within Native/tribal communities was often done through sacred ceremony. Joseph Epes Brown notes that the names of individuals "imply relationship, protection, favor, and influence from the source of the named. Names indicate affiliation, connote power, and have sacred import."[10] The assertion of one's name, especially one's tribal community name, is especially important as tribal communities often acquired names imposed on them by competing communities, by the federal government, or by other non-community members.

A vocabulary that is reflective of indigenous thought respects indigenous history. When asked, we reply: indigenous people know who they are.[11] Haunani-Kay Trask offers this definition: "indigenous peoples are defined in terms of collective aboriginal occupation prior to colonial settlement."[12] She further explains how association with the land is a key element in understanding the difference between indigenous and settler populations:

> Unlike settlers in Hawai'i (*haole*, Asians, and others), who *voluntarily* gave up the nationality of their homelands when they be-

[9] Frank Stewart, Kareva Mateata-Allain, and Alexander Dale Mawyer, *Varua Tupu: New Writing From French Polynesia* (Honolulu: University of Hawai'I Press, 2006), xii.

[10] Joseph Epes Brown, *Animals of the Soul* (Rockport, MA: Element Books, 1997), rev. ed., 67, in Mary Jane Lupton, *James Welch: A Critical Companion* (Westport, CT: Greenwood Press, 2004), *The American Indian Experience*, Greenwood Publishing Group, http://aie.greenwood.com// doc.aspx?fileID=GR2725&chapterID=GR2725417&path=books/green wood (accessed 2 June 2009).

[11] Loriene Roy, "Indigenous Matters in Library and Information Science: An Evolving Ecology," *Focus in International Library and Information Work* 40:2 (July 2009): 8-12.

[12] Haunani-Kay Trask, *From a Native Daughter: Colonialism and Sovereignty in Hawai'i,* 2nd ed. (Honolulu: University of Hawai'i Press, 1999), 33.

came permanent residents of Hawai'i, Hawaiians had their nationality *forcibly changed in their own homeland* (emphasis in original).[13]

We can see the connection to land in other discussions of indigenous community naming. Frank Stewart, Kareva Mateata-Allain,
and Alexander Dale Mawyer describe how Ma'ohi, the name for
the indigenous peoples of the Society Islands, also reflects life from
the earth:

> Ohi refers to a sprout which has already taken root, securing it-
> self with a certain autonomy of life, all the while being linked to
> the mother stem. From a sprout, an ohi, tracing back its roots,
> one always gets to a trunk. Ma'ohi is the community of all those
> who claim to be of the same past, culture and language, which
> constitute the common trunk and which still have the same des-
> tiny.[14]

Naming is at the center of international human rights for indigenous peoples as well. The UN's definition of indigenous peoples similarly focuses on a connection to land:

> Indigenous communities, peoples and nations are those which,
> having a historical continuity with pre-invasion and pre-colonial
> societies that developed on their territories, consider themselves
> distinct from other sectors of the societies now prevailing in
> those territories, or parts of them. They form at present non-
> dominant sectors of society and are determined to preserve, de-
> velop and transmit to future generations their ancestral territo-
> ries, and their ethnic identity, as the basis of their continued exis-
> tence as peoples, in accordance with their own cultural patterns,
> social institutions and legal systems.[15]

Significantly, the UN definition relies on indigenous history related
to land claims, "having a historical continuity with pre-invasion and
pre-colonial societies that developed on their territories," and on
indigenous self-identification, "consider[ing] themselves distinct

---

[13] Ibid., 30.
[14] Stewart, *Varua Tupu*, xii.
[15] Stavenhagen, "Cultural Rights," 105.

from other sectors of the societies." Self-naming is, ultimately, inseparable from self-determination.[16]

The naming of the Declaration of Rights of Indigenous Peoples marks a shift in international human rights. In early drafts, the document bore the name Declaration of Rights of Indigenous People, and Stavenhagen explains that the difference between *people* and *peoples* "is of considerable political importance to indigenous organizations. International law does not accord the right to self-determination to indigenous peoples (nor does it to minorities), and therefore states discourage the use of the term 'indigenous peoples' in international legal instruments."[17] Since Stavenhagen's writing from 2001, the passage of the Declaration of Rights of Indigenous Peoples declares for indigenous peoples the right of self-determination. Article 3 reads: "Indigenous peoples have the right to self-determination. By virtue of that right they freely determine their political status and freely pursue their economic, social, and cultural development." Indigenous rights to self-naming, to self-determination, shift previous documents' emphases on an individual's participation in a national culture to a collective right to cultural development. This shift forms the basis for an indigenous reading of cultural rights in librarianship where librarians can consider their user communities to not only include individual patrons but also tribal groups that are defined, in part, by their common cultural expressions such as language and performance arts. In this chapter we use the words indigenous peoples and Native peoples to refer to the first peoples, although we are aware that other individuals or communities may prefer to use a different word or even consider the words indigenous or Native to be pejorative.

### How Have Librarians Participated in Tribal History?

In the nineteenth century, Manifest Destiny was a U.S. federal policy governing treatment of indigenous peoples. A belief in the superiority of American warfare and philosophies led to the settler

---

[16] Cobo, José Martinez, Special Rapporteur. *Study of the Problem of Discrimination against Indigenous Populations – Volume 5: Conclusions, Proposals, and Recommendations*, UN Doc E/CN.4/Sub.2/1986/7/Add.4 (March 1987), 379.

[17] Stavenhagen, "Cultural Rights," 107.

populace moving west while suppressing the cultures of the people who lived on the land they "found" along the way. This philosophy coincided with the golden age of public library development. A look at confluences of library and tribal histories suggests that librarians' contributions to national campaigns for individual rights have been at the cost of indigenous librarianship and cultures. Meanwhile, indigenous librarians' articulation of collective rights offers an opportunity for librarians at large to take collective responsibility for intervening in systems of oppression.

The work of libraries during the field's founding years articulated a faith in a singular American ideal similar to that espoused by a U.S. government intent on destroying tribal cultures whose values differed from American individualism. LIS scholar Jonathan Furner describes the work of public libraries in the 19th century as "a tool for the promotion of the interests of the ruling classes," in part, "inculcating in new immigrants the morals of the American who is 'sober, righteous, conservative, patient, devout.'"[18] ALA was founded in Philadelphia during the U.S. Centennial year of 1876, the same year that the Battle of the Little Big Horn took place between the Sioux and Cheyenne and the U.S. Seventh Cavalry in present day Montana. The death of General George Armstrong Custer and 224 other men along the Little Big Horn River remains the most well known battle of the Indian Wars.[19] In 1887, while Melville Dewey established the first library school at Columbia University, the U.S. government continued to contract with boarding schools across the nation. The system of boarding schools sought cultural genocide through assimilation of indigenous peoples. Andrea Smith, Cherokee activist and scholar, explains, "At-

---

[18] Jonathan Furner, "Dewey Deracialized: A Critical Race-Theoretic Perspective," *Knowledge Organization* 34 (2007): 144-68, 151.

[19] John M. Coward, W. Joseph Campbell, David A. Copeland, "LITTLE BIGHORN (MONTANA), 1876," in *The Greenwood Library of American War Reporting Volume 4, The Indian Wars & The Spanish-American War* (Westport, CT: Greenwood Press, 2005), *The American Indian Experience*, Greenwood Publishing Group, http://aie.greenwood.com//doc.aspx?fileID=GR2990-3201&chapterID=GR2990-3201&path=chunkbook (accessed 2 June 2009).

tendance at these boarding schools was mandatory, and children from tribes across the U.S. were forcibly taken from their homes for the majority of the year. Parents who resisted were imprisoned."[20] Also in 1887, the U.S. government passed the Dawes Act, the federal law of allotment that divided tribal lands into smaller plots assigned to families, considered to be a failure from the Native standpoint since it led to loss of homeland areas and rewarded individual ownership over collective caretaking of land.[21] The first exhibit of library materials at the Columbian Exhibition in Chicago in 1893 took place three years after the 1890 Massacre at Wounded Knee in present day South Dakota.[22]

U.S. librarianship's turn to protecting freedoms of expression began as the U.S. government increased its attempt to disperse and dissolve tribal identity; founded in individualism, both individual freedom of expression and U.S. policy against tribal identity suppressed indigenous cultures. The adoption of the Library Bill of Rights in 1939 occurred five years after the Indian Reorganization Act was passed, repealing the Dawes Act and promoting new tribal government models.[23] In 1953, the ALA adopted the Freedom to

---

[20] Andrea Smith, *Conquest: Sexual Violence and American Indian Genocide* (Cambridge, MA: South End Press, 2005), 37.

[21] James S. Olson, Mark Baxter, Jason M. Tetzloff, and Darren Pierson, "DAWES ACT OF 1887," in *Encyclopedia of American Indian Civil Rights* (Westport, CT: Greenwood Press, 1997), *The American Indian Experience*, Greenwood Publishing Group, http://aie.greenwood.com//doc.aspx?fileID=GR9338&chapterID=GR9338-1080&path=encyclopedias/greenwood (accessed 2 June 2009).

[22] James S. Olson, Mark Baxter, Jason M. Tetzloff, and Darren Pierson, "WOUNDED KNEE (1890)," in *Encyclopedia of American Indian Civil Rights* (Westport, CT: Greenwood Press, 1997), *The American Indian Experience*, Greenwood Publishing Group, http://aie.greenwood.com//doc.aspx?fileID=GR9338&chapterID=GR9338-4662&path=encyclopedias/greenwood (accessed 2 June 2009).

[23] James S. Olson, Mark Baxter, Jason M. Tetzloff, and Darren Pierson, "INDIAN REORGANIZATION ACT OF 1934," in *Encyclopedia of American Indian Civil Rights* (Westport, CT: Greenwood Press, 1997), *The American Indian Experience*, Greenwood Publishing Group,

Read Statement just over one month before the U.S. Congress adopted House Concurrent Resolution 108, which, as Wilma Mankiller, Principal Chief of the Cherokee Nation, recalls in her memoir, "withdrew the federal commitment for Indian people."[24] This resolution began the termination movement. Utah Senator Arthur V. Watkins, then head of the Senate subcommittee on Indian affairs, "labeled termination as 'the Indian freedom program,'"[25] because it ended federal services and protection for tribes and native communities. Mankiller, a child during this period of displacement, explains, "The passage and implementation of termination bills during the 1950s shocked many Indian leaders, who immediately understood that the United States government again intended to destroy tribal governments. Many of them also realized that the government intended to break up native communities and put tribal land on the market by abolishing its status as nontaxable trust land."[26] These policies resulted in displacement and loss of self-determination.[27] Amidst the federal government's termination of tribes and relocation of many American Indians to urban settings, the U.S. government emphasized libraries' support for the

---

http://aie.greenwood.com//doc.aspx?fileID=GR9338&chapterID=GR9 338-2136&path=encyclopedias/greenwood (accessed 2 June 2009).

[24] Wilma Mankiller and Michael Wallis, *Mankiller: A Chief and Her People* (New York: St. Martin's Press, 1993), 67.

[25] Ibid., 68.

[26] Ibid., 68.

[27] James S. Olson, Mark Baxter, Jason M. Tetzloff, and Darren Pierson, "TERMINATION," in *Encyclopedia of American Indian Civil Rights* (Westport, CT: Greenwood Press, 1997), *The American Indian Experience*, Greenwood Publishing Group, http://aie.greenwood.com// doc.aspx?fileID=GR9338&chapterID=GR9338-4067&path= encyclopedias/greenwood (accessed June 2, 2009); James S. Olson, Mark Baxter, Jason M. Tetzloff, and Darren Pierson, "RELOCATION," in *Encyclopedia of American Indian Civil Rights* (Westport, CT: Greenwood Press, 1997), *The American Indian Experience*. Greenwood Publishing Group, http://aie.greenwood.com//doc.aspx?fileID=GR9338& chapterID=GR9338-3653&path=encyclopedias/greenwood (accessed 2 June 2009).

individual American ideal of education and achievement when it passed the Library Services Act in 1956. These selected points show a distinct divergence in primacy between American librarians and Native peoples. Prior to the late 1960s, Native peoples were primarily trying to survive the vagaries of ongoing colonialism, while the U.S. government and public libraries simultaneously articulated a national culture of individualism. Indigenous concerns and those of librarians begin to converge in the 1970s after pressure from the American Indian Movement. During the Civil Rights and Red Power Movement days of the 1970s, the American Library Association began to support indigenous self-determination within the ALA. The organization established a Subcommittee on Library Services for American Indians, an ALA unit that continues to this day. Several years later, in 1979, the American Indian Library Association, an affiliate of the American Library Association, was founded.[28]

Today, many events and developments point to the evolution of a burgeoning area of indigenous librarianship—the establishment of indigenous library organizations in Aotearoa/New Zealand and Australia in the 1990s, the International Indigenous Librarians Forum that has taken place every other year since 1999, and national Tribal Archives, Libraries, and Museums conferences starting in 2003. This attention to libraries and the cultural record is taking place during a time when many tribal communities have developed more diverse economies and their communities are looking beyond basic survival into cultural heritage initiatives, including indigenous language revival and the construction of cultural heritage edifices such as the National Museum of the American Indian.

An understanding of the connections between the histories of librarianship and U.S. colonial policy calls on librarians to shift away from an individualist ideology. Susan Dion (Lenape/Potawatami), professor of education at York University, has developed a pedagogical practice she calls "braiding history" which allows hearing and acknowledgement of indigenous histories and

---

28 "About AILA," *American Indian Library Association,*
http://www.ailanet.org/about/index.htm (accessed 2 June 2009).

experience in order to end violence against indigenous peoples. Dion explains, "Canadians 'refuse to know' that the racism that fuelled colonization sprang from a system that benefits all non-Aboriginal people, not just the European settlers of long ago. This refusal to know is comforting: it supports an understanding of racism as an act of individuals, not of a system."[29] Only by refusing to know about the systematic violence against indigenous communities and cultures can librarians continue to support a purely individual right to expression. This individualist nation-building, Stavenhagen points out, "means that the various ethnic and cultural groups who for one historical reason or another find themselves living within the defined borders of an internationally recognized state, are expected to give up parts of their cultural identity to either adopt the values of the dominant or majority groups, or else to mix and create something entirely new."[30] By insisting on individual rights to the exclusion of group rights, we participate in suppressing cultures. In order to work against this suppression, librarians must accept the collective responsibility required by recognizing collective rights.

**Participating in the Cultural Life of the Community: Indigenous Peoples' Cultural Life in Libraries**

This section takes into account the first paragraph of Article 27 to grapple with what it would mean to ensure indigenous peoples' "right freely to participate in the cultural life of the community." The history and syntax of Article 27 indicates that it supports a single culture of a single community; this vision of one amalgamated culture, however, results in silencing minority and indigenous cultures within the nation. Ultimately, Stavenhagen surmises, "Hegemonic cultural groups who have the ability or power to define the national culture then expect all other groups to conform to this model, even if that means, in the long run, the destruction of

---

[29] Susan Dion, *Braiding Histories: Learning from Aboriginal Peoples' Experiences and Perspectives* (Vancouver: University of British Columbia Press, 2009), 56-7.
[30] Stavenhagen, "Cultural Rights," 96.

other cultures."[31] Drafting cultural rights for a homogenous public, then, results in librarians' complicity in silencing marginalized groups within cultural institutions. Toni Samek observes that librarians and other cultural workers "have both consciously and unconsciously participated in tasks that have resulted in concessions, absences, omissions, biases, negations (e.g. misrepresentation of racialised and immigrant cultures), broken cultural protocols, and disconnects 'between the way peoples are presented in mainstream' culture, 'including library materials' and the way people 'present themselves and their own culture.'"[32] In order to support indigenous peoples' access to the cultural rights of Article 27, librarians must look beyond the western individualist formulation of UDHR to include collective rights to participation in the cultural life for multiple communities.

International human rights documents offer and imply multiple definitions of culture; it is important to note that different definitions of culture are implicated in different economic and social value systems, therefore there is not a single universal definition. Librarians, as critical readers, must understand different cultural significances in different situations and communities. Cindy Holder, scholar of philosophy at the University of Victoria, traces the challenge of indigenous epistemologies to western definitions of culture:

> Historically, culture has been treated as an object in international documents. One consequence of this is that cultural rights in international law have been understood as rights of access and consumption. Recently, an alternative conception of culture, and of what cultural rights protect, has emerged from international documents treating indigenous peoples. Within these documents culture is treated as an activity rather than as a good.[33]

---

[31] Ibid., 96.

[32] Toni Samek, *Librarianship and Human Rights: A Twenty-First Century Guide* (Oxford: Chandos Publishing, 2007), 13-14.

[33] Cindy Holder, "Culture as an Activity and Human Right: An Important Advance for Indigenous Peoples and International Law," *Alternatives: Global, Local, Political* 33:1 (2008): 7-28, 7.

If we extend Holder's line of interpretation, rights to objects or conditions form a part of cultural rights not because the object is a cultural product but because, as Stavenhagen argues, "access to and control over them is necessary for indigenous peoples to *be cultural on terms of their own choosing*" [emphasis in original].[34] While library collections emphasize collections of material, librarians must see indigenous culture as both the cultural object, including literature, and the process of creating and using cultural objects; that is, librarians must engage with how indigenous peoples choose to be cultural. From this perspective of multiple cultural practices, we can begin to examine and deconstruct the culture of western library collection management.

Through building and providing access to their collections, librarians support the spirit of the first paragraph of Article 27: they affirm free participation, enjoyment, and sharing in the cultural life of the community. A critical reading of the historical context of Article 27 cautions librarians to examine whether they support a single homogenous culture and to explore how they can shift to support the multiple cultures in our communities. Library collections represent primacy and ownership. Building library collections is held as the domain of the librarian, specifically the professional librarian who completes graduate level coursework in collection development and management. Belief in one's ability to build a collection was felt to be equivalent to a religious calling. Similarly, librarians who step into existing collections often regard the collections as sacrosanct, built under the expertise of their predecessors. With knowledge of collection development processes, and armed with a strong collection development policy, a librarian might feel justified in adding any item to the collection. Once acquired, cataloged and processed, the intention or use of an item is then outside of the control of library staff.

Selection of material by a librarian for a collection confers on that material a sense of legitimacy. Modern librarians have employed the Library Bill of Rights as a starting point for providing their publics with wanted, valued, and useful information. ALA

---

[34] Stavenhagen, "Cultural Rights," 19.

Council has adopted Interpretations of the Library Bill of Rights to areas including electronic information, free access to library resources by patrons under legal age, opposition to labeling content, and opposition to restricting access to library resources.[35] McCook and Phenix cite evidence of librarians' professional support for human rights in the language of key ALA documents such as the Library Bill of Rights and the ALA Code of Ethics and in the endorsement of Article 19 by ALA and by IFLA, the International Federation of Library Associations.[36]

Librarians are further called on to build collections that reflect community needs. They provide balanced collections through a process outlined in their selection policy. This policy may include an explanation of collection diversity. Such diversity extends to acquiring material written or created by indigenous peoples. Librarians' acquisition policies can support or suppress diverse literature; therefore, in order to advocate for indigenous peoples' cultural rights, librarians must actively support indigenous literature as well as indigenous use of that literature. Two central issues for supporting indigenous cultural life in the library are inclusion of indigenous literature in the collection and respecting indigenous protocols. Some literature may be subject to traditional protocols limiting its use. The thought that a library might hold an item in its collection that harbors secret knowledge may be a startling concept for librarians. In contrast, indigenous people may view their interactions with people and the natural world as governed by certain behavior that they call protocol, an etiquette that has evolved over centuries. Protocol refers to the "spoken and unspoken rules for how to treat others"[37] and is applied to the everyday activities of

---

[35]American Library Association, "Interpretation of the Library Bill of Rights," *American Library Association*, http://www.ala.org/ala/aboutala/offices/oif/statementspols/statementsif/interpretations/default.cfm (4 June 2009).

[36] McCook and Phenix, "Human Rights and Librarians."

[37] Alice Nash and Christoph Strobel, "Daily Life among the Algonkians," in *Daily Life of Native Americans from Post-Columbian through Nineteenth-Century America* (Westport, CT:Greenwood Press, 2006), *The American Indian Experience*, Greenwood Publishing Group

introducing oneself and greeting others as well as to ceremony and
performing special actions. These protocols can also apply to spoken words such as stories, to the capturing of stories in print, to
images such as those recorded in photographs, and to artifacts.
Full support for a collective right to cultural life requires librarian advocacy to protect the cultural rights of marginalized populations. Librarians and scholars Shiraz Durrani and Elizabeth Smallwood explain that the too-general language of the ALA and intellectual freedom advocacy for "neutrality" policies result not in actual (impossible) neutrality, but in a collection and practice defined
by corporate interests. Globally, they argue, libraries have "become
increasingly isolated from the majority of people in their local
communities. Forces of corporate globalization then push them
even further from their communities by offering to save staff time
and mental effort by supplying pre-packaged 'best sellers,' guaranteed to meet the wants of 30% of the population—and to boost
the profit margins of transnational publishers and booksellers."[38]
These library scholars point out that in the name of free market
"neutrality," libraries are limiting literary diversity. Rather than ab-
solute neutrality, which, in reality, favors a mainstream few, communication scholar Laura Stein supports Durrani and Smallwood's
argument against giving in to the market, explaining, "Media markets also systematically disfavor unpopular and minority viewpoints."[39] Librarians, as keepers of media archives and distribution
centers, support multiple communities' cultural lives when they
eschew free market neutrality and turn, instead, to supporting diverse cultures. Similarly envisioning her work as "a direct challenge
to the notion of library neutrality, especially in the present context
of war, revolution, social change and global market fundamental-

---

http://aie.greenwood.com//doc.aspx?fileID=GR3515&chapterID=GR3
515-170&path=books/greenwood (accessed 2 June 2009).
[38] Shiraz Durrani and Elizabeth Smallwood, "The Professional Is Political:
Redefining the Social Role of Public Libraries," in *Questioning Library Neutrality: Essays from Progressive Librarian*, ed. Alison Lewis (Duluth, MN: Library Juice Press, 2008), 119-140, 120.
[39] Laura Stein, *Speech Rights in America: The First Amendment, Democracy, and
the Media* (Urbana: University of Illinois Press, 2006), 47.

ism," Samek points out that such a move towards activism as part of library advocacy generates "the development of more humanistic (and less techno-managerial) library and information work."[40] This chapter, then, offers a pathway to a practice of critical librarianship that supports indigenous peoples' cultural life in libraries. Indigenous literature in the library changes the work of the library, because indigenous literature, even with a single author, claims participation in collective storytelling and requires that readers take responsibility for our participation in a collective relationship either as (if the reader is indigenous) or with indigenous peoples. In Lois Beardslee's fictional narrative *The Women's Warrior Society*, she repeatedly envisions indigenous women reclaiming the space of the library. In several chapters, the library becomes, under the watch of the women warriors, a sacred sweatlodge:

> The keeper of the eastern door, she takes off her glasses and rubs them with the corner of her shirt. She is careful not to scratch them with her long, wolf-woman claws. She spreads the papers out on the table. They are contemporary stories, modern history, study after study about racism in education. They come from scholarly books. They come from scholarly journals. They come from Indians.[41]

This kind of storytelling, and its emphasis on indigenous authorship – "They come from Indians" – constructs an indigenous community's cultural life. Cherokee literary scholar Jace Weaver calls this concept communitism, a combination of community and activism:

> Literature is communitist to the extent that it has a proactive commitment to Native community, including what I term the 'wider community' of Creation itself. In communities that have too often been fractured and rendered dysfunctional by the effects of more than 500 years of colonialism, to promote com-

---

[40] Samek, *Librarianship and Human Rights*, 7.
[41] Lois Beardslee, *The Women's Warrior Society* (Tucson: University of Arizona Press, 2008), 58.

munitist values means to participate in the healing of the grief and sense of exile felt by Native communities.[42]

For Weaver, then, not only is the authorship communal, but the literature is also a vital practice, a way of being cultural, in the continued cultural life of the community. In order to support this literature through distribution, librarians must not only seek out and order this literature, but they must also respect cultural uses of the literature.

Librarians might be unfamiliar with tribal cultural protocol and with how it applies to traditional knowledge expressions that they might house in their collections. For example, such protocol may restrict certain knowledge, such as cultural stories, to a certain time of year. Patty Loew reminds librarians planning storytelling events that Native communities in and around the Great Lakes region might tell stories only when the ground is covered with snow.[43] One rationale for this protocol is that all features of the earth are living. If stories are told near an open window, they are carried by the wind to the grasses and trees and eventually to the person or being featured in the stories. In this case, storytelling becomes the equivalent of gossip and can do damage. Another explanation for telling stories only during the winter is that winter was a season when families stayed inside. Storytelling during other seasons might interrupt the activities associated with food gathering. Additionally, tribal community members may have access to material only if they are of a certain gender, age, or affiliated with a subsection of the community such as a clan. Some access may be transferred over time and only to those who have inherited access. The Society for American Archivists (SAA) also observes that some cultural items have a life cycle and, according to their nature, may not have been intended to exist or be held in a collection forever.[44]

[42] Jace Weaver, *That the People Might Live: Native American Literatures and Native American Community* (New York: Oxford UP, 1997), xiii.
[43] Patty Loew, *We Shall Remain: An Event Kit For Libraries* (Boston: WGBH-Boston, 2008), 6.
[44] Society for American Archivists, "Protocols for Native Archival Materials," 2007, http://www2.nau.edu/libnap-p/protocols.html (accessed 4 June 2009).

Librarians schooled in the philosophy of equal and open access may be confused about the difference between cultural protection and limiting access. To the librarian schooled in the strong tenets of intellectual freedom this may sound less like courtesy and more like censorship. Human rights scholarship reminds us that cultural rights must include different communities' definitions of culture: "The right to culture implies the respect for the cultural values of groups and individuals by others who may not share these values; it means the right to be different. How else are we to interpret the fundamental freedoms of thought, of expression, of opinion, of belief, that are enshrined in the Universal Declaration of Human Rights,"[45] Stavenhagen asks. That is, necessary decisions limiting access must respect the right of collective groups to be cultural. Since culture is not only the object (the book) but is also the act (the writing and the use of the book), limiting the general public's right to access all indigenous literature all year round actually preserves indigenous peoples' right to be cultural and still allows limited use of the material by the general public. However, allowing unlimited use of literature that falls under protocol restriction infringes on indigenous peoples' cultural rights since it neglects the etiquette or protocol that prescribe the actions associated with living an indigenous life.

Discussions of traditional knowledge expression emphasize the need for librarians to work closely with tribal community members. This may spark a feeling of fear of loss of autonomy on the part of librarians. While most librarians have experience working with a community advisory group, such as a library board of trustees, these relationships are built over time and often have a narrow focus. The possibility of working with another community with different perspectives and aims directed toward library collections and services may be off putting. As stated earlier, members of western cultures, especially Americans with unearned privilege, such as white or class privilege, are not accustomed to being told that they cannot do something. This relates not only to the right to purchase

---

[45] Stavenhagen, "Cultural Rights," 93.

or request information but also to do with information what one
will.

While the Aboriginal and Torres Strait Islander Library Information and Resource Network (ATSILIRN) Protocols note that
the best advice for librarians does not support censoring material
("material now considered offensive or inappropriate still form part
of the historical record") they also point out that "an item need not
be on open access to everyone just because it has been published."[46] To aid in identifying potentially problematic material,
Australian librarians have discussed the possibility of developing a
national database that lists publications that are known to contain
content that indigenous peoples would consider sacred or secret.
One element of access to traditional cultural knowledge concerns
ways to protect indigenous users. While the ALA opposes labeling
of library materials, indigenous peoples may ask librarians to help
them become aware of specialized content so that they might avoid
it. In Australia, these recommendations "might involve labels,
notes in the catalogue indicating that the contents are 'For initiated
males only' or include 'Women's business.'"[47] The SAA protocols
provide examples of the types of materials that might be found in
archives that are of a sacred nature including photographs, films,
recordings and their written transcripts, maps, and published material on family genealogies or religious ceremony. In some tribal li-
braries/archives, readers are notified that tribes do not endorse
specific publications. At this point it is important to remember
what the SAA Protocols remind us: a very small portion of the cultural material in a collection is likely to be of a sacred or secret nature.

While librarians might be unaware of Native peoples and the
expression of traditional knowledge, Native peoples might also be
unfamiliar with the professional tenets of librarianship as well as
the policies under which libraries operate. To some Native people,

---

[46] Aboriginal and Torres Strait Islander Library Information and Resource
Network, "ATSILIRN Protocols,"
http://www1.aiatsis.gov.au/atsilirn/protocols.atsilirn.asn.au/index0c51.ht
ml?option=com_frontpage&Itemid=1/ (accessed 2 June 2009).
[47] ATSILIRN, "ATSILIRN Protocols."

a library may be perceived as an extension of damaging federal policies. Rooms stocked with English language text may feel oppressive in cultures where community culture and language were suppressed. The Australian library organization devoted to library resources and services for Aboriginal and Torres Strait Islanders Library workers reminds us that Native people may feel intimidated in libraries, especially since their families might not have a tradition of using these institutions.[48] Librarians may have to endeavor to build trust in such communities. Approaches to building trust include demonstrating long-term commitment, including Native peoples in decision-making, and working to recruit and support indigenous library students and librarians. Similarly, librarians and Native peoples can learn to work productively through approaches that involve shared authority. While such collaborations might feel unfamiliar and even daunting, Alicia J. Rouverol reminds us that "It's precisely when we want to give up on collaboration that we most need to return to dialogue, try to listen, and open our thinking to new strategies."[49]

**Protecting Moral and Material Interests: Learning from Indigenous Librarianship**

Lois Beardslee's library-sweatlodge offers a model for public library practice of cultural rights of indigenous peoples:

> The flimsy metal walls of the library-sweatlodge bulge and vacillate. Books and scholarly journals are exchanged, and coping mechanisms are crocheted like thick winter sweaters, heaped upon an accumulating pile of experience and determination and competence. There are books, letters, treaties, court cases, baby booties, and beaded moccasins. There are dictionaries and computers and fishing rights and baby blankets and textbooks and old sweetgrass baskets heaped upon the table of power.[50]

---

[48] Ibid.
[49] Rouverol, Alicia J., "Collaborative Oral History in a Correctional Setting: Promise and Pitfalls," *The Oral History Review* 30:1 (Winter/Spring 2003): 61-85.
[50] Beardslee, *The Women's Warrior Society*, 62.

Central to indigenous cultural practice in her library are self-determination and property rights, indigenous identity and agency within the library, and indigenous narrative power to reshape the library space. The final section of this chapter offers tools for librarians to use to claim human rights as library protocol.

## Indigenous cultural property rights

The language of the second paragraph of Article 27, just as in the first, roots it in a western individualistic tradition: "Everyone has the right to the protection of the moral and material interests resulting from any scientific, literary or artistic production of which he is the author." Intellectual property rights, the core of the article, are central to indigenous cultural rights; looking to indigenous rights documents allows an expanded reading of Article 27 and a call for librarians' support. Dutch human rights scholar Cees Hamelink explains the western free market basis for current interpretations of intellectual property law: "Since the protection of intellectual property defines knowledge as private property, it can function as an effective right to monopolize control which restricts the free flow of ideas and knowledge."[51] In the face of these monopolies, Stamatopoulou points out that international trade law "has not managed to accommodate the protection of traditional knowledge and cultural heritage of indigenous peoples. The immense financial interests involved are considered to be a major reason."[52] That is, allowing or supporting monopolies (including mega-publishers and distributors) can actually impede the support of indigenous peoples' participation in cultural life. Since, theoretically, library practice is not motivated by economic gain, librarians are in a unique position to create a model for supporting a diverse literature and, in particular, indigenous peoples' cultural practices.

The Declaration on the Rights of Indigenous Peoples has set out a new system for intellectual property rights. Alexandra Xanthaki, international human rights and legal scholar, gestures to-

---

[51] Cees J. Hamelink, "Cultural Rights in the Global Village," in *Cultural Rights in a Global World*, ed. Anura Goonasekera, Cees Hamelink, and Venkat Iyer (Singapore: Eastern Universities Press, 2003), 19.
[52] Stamatopoulou, "Why Cultural Rights Now ?"

wards the significance of including intellectual property rights in the Declaration, "since the Western preoccupation with individual expression that underpins these rights [is] at odds with indigenous collective experiences of cultural expression."[53] The Declaration instead writes intellectual property rights "in a manner that implies the creation of a *sui generis* system."[54] Article 31 of the Declaration includes indigenous autonomy over cultural property: "Indigenous peoples have the right to maintain, control, protect and develop their cultural heritage, traditional knowledge and traditional cultural expressions." The Declaration, in connection with UDHR Article 27, confirms that librarians must look to indigenous policies to inform library collection and circulation policies.

One such landmark policy is the "Mataatua Declaration on Cultural and Intellectual Property Rights of Indigenous People," developed at the First International Conference on the Cultural and Intellectual Property Rights of Indigenous Peoples held in Aotearoa/New Zealand in 1993, the year the United Nations proclaimed the International Year of the World's Indigenous Peoples. This document includes ten recommendations for indigenous peoples, fourteen for states, national, and international agencies, and five for the United Nations and is strongly worded to demand action on the part of indigenous peoples and/or the libraries, archives, museums or other institutions that hold and provide access to indigenous material culture. It states, in part, that "We ... declare that all forms of discrimination and exploitation of Indigenous Peoples, indigenous knowledge and indigenous cultural and intellectual property rights must cease."[55] As stated in the ATSILIRN Protocols, librarians are the key agents responsible for this change: "Information agencies will be proactive in the role of educator, promoting awareness of Aboriginal and Torres Strait Is-

---

[53] Alexandra Xanthaki, "Indigenous Rights in International Law over the Last 10 Years and Future Developments," *Melbourne Journal of International Law* 10:1 (2009): 27-37, 31.
[54] Ibid., 31.
[55] "Mataatua Declaration on Cultural and Intellectual Property Rights of Indigenous People," http://ankn.uaf.edu/IKS/mataatua.html (accessed 2 June 2009).

lander peoples, cultures and issues among non-indigenous people."[56] Statements such as these, located within broader based
statements, affirm the role of those working in institutions to serve
as non-neutral custodians.

At their heart, these documents and others address cultural materials and/or content as well as their ownership and use. They introduce the deeper meaning of cultural rights. The SAA Protocols,
for example, note that the ethical ground under which cultural material was acquired by archives has changed over time, as have notions of access, and call on libraries and archives to acknowledge
that Native communities hold the primary rights for their associated cultural expressions. The Mataatua Declaration asks for recognition of indigenous peoples as the exclusive owners of their
property—whether it is cultural property or intellectual property.
The "Guidelines for Respecting Cultural Knowledge" calls on
authors and illustrators to "arrange for copyright authority and roy-
alties to be retained or shared by the person or community from
which the cultural information originated."[57]

There is also a reminder that libraries, and especially archives,
might also be involved in discussions regarding copying material
with indigenous content as well as lending through services such as
interlibrary loan. Similarly, they might also be called on to return
original documents, a process of repatriation, especially when materials are obtained through theft or other immoral means. Their
role might extend to assisting Native communities in the long-term
care and preservation of such items. The SAA Protocols also suggest that libraries and archives return materials to tribes if holding
said items is outside of the scope of the institution's collection
policies.

---

[56] ATSILIRN, "ATSILIRN Protocols."
[57] Assembly of Alaska Native Educators, *Guidelines for Respecting Cultural
Knowledge.* http://www.ankn.uaf.edu/publications/Knowledge.pdf (accessed 2 June 2009), 6.

## Librarians' identity and indigenous agency

Since a key part of indigenous peoples' cultural rights is indigenous control over indigenous cultural practices and creations, it is important that non-indigenous librarians look to the leadership of indigenous librarians and foster the additional recruitment, training, and hiring of indigenous librarians. Daniel Heath Justice, Cherokee literary scholar, articulates the importance of his scholarly focus on Cherokee voices, "an exercise of intellectual sovereignty and a matter of ethical accountability: Cherokees are in the first and best place to speak about who we are and what's important to us; to deny these voices, or to marginalize them in favor of those whose assumed authority is embedded within the ideologies of colonialism, is to add strength to the Eurowestern assimilationist directive from within."[58] The same holds true in librarianship; libraries cannot support indigenous peoples' cultural rights without including indigenous librarians and library consultants in shaping the space and work of the library. If it seems to some non-indigenous librarians almost impossible to develop relationships with indigenous communities, librarians, or advocates, feminist philosopher Linda Alcoff emphasizes that obstacles do not absolve non-indigenous librarians from seeking indigenous partners. "Often the possibility of dialogue is left unexplored or inadequately pursued by more privileged persons," Alcoff cautions; "Spaces in which it may seem as if it is impossible to engage in dialogic encounters need to be transformed in order to do so."[59] Thus far, this chapter has modeled the work of looking to print resources as a foundation for dialogue on indigenous human rights. The following ALA and indigenous librarians' documents serve as guides for building dialogue with indigenous communities around cultural life in libraries.

Two of the six major initiatives in ALA's next strategic plan, "ALA Ahead to 2010," address issues of interest for indigenous librarians. These are the statements that "ALA plays a key role in

---

[58] Daniel Heath Justice, *Our Fire Survives the Storm: A Cherokee Literary History* (Minneapolis: University of Minnesota Press, 2006), 209.
[59] Linda Alcoff, "The Problem of Speaking for Others," *Cultural Critique* (Winter 1991-2): 5-32, 30.

the formulation of national and international policies and standards that affect library and information services" and "ALA is a leader in recruiting and developing a highly qualified and diverse library work force."[60]

There are other relevant ALA policy statements. In 1990/91, ALA Council adopted Article 19 of the United Nations' Universal Declaration of Human Rights into ALA Policy.[61] ALA's one policy that specifically mentions indigenous peoples is Policy 59.3, "Indian Themes." Here, ALA acknowledges a professional responsibility to consider culturally appropriate imagery in library services: "ALA and its divisions are encouraged to consult with the American Indian Library Association before using or creating Indian theme illustrations, graphics, programs, or publicity."[62] While this policy might appear to diverge from considerations of Native peoples and their cultural property, it brings the issue to the level of the librarian practitioner—calling on him or her to avoid stereotypes and misrepresentation.

In an era of developing standards and professional competency documents, librarians have also been involved in the creation of principles that guide their interactions with indigenous peoples and expressions of their culture. Some documents were developed by professional organizations while others stemmed from gatherings of individuals representing various professional communities. As members of the SAA have pointed out, there is a need to examine the relationships that have existed between tribes and those staffing libraries and archives.[63]

Some guidelines suggest decision-making processes such as appointing tribal community members to play active, participatory

---

[60] ALA, "ALA Ahead to 2010 Strategic Plan," *ALA Handbook of Organization* (Chicago: ALA, 2008), ix-x.

[61] ALA, "[Policy] 58.5, Article 19 of the United Nations' Universal Declaration of Human Rights," *ALA Handbook of Organization* (Chicago: ALA, 2008), 11-12.

[62] ALA, "[Policy] 59.3, Indian Themes," *ALA Handbook of Organization* (Chicago: ALA, 2008), 72.

[63] SAA, "Protocols for Native Archival Materials."

roles on library boards and/or relevant library committees. In many cases, tribal elders play a vital role. "Guidelines for Respecting Cultural Knowledge" provides an excellent definition for Elder: "the identification of 'Elders' as culture-bearers is not simply a matter of chronological age, but a function of the respect accorded to individuals in each community who exemplify the values and lifeways of the local culture and who possess the wisdom and willingness to pass their knowledge on to future generations."[64] Thus, there are true Elders, Junior Elders, and just plain old people who have not assumed the responsibilities or earned the qualification to be recognized as an Elder. Elders can participate through an Elders' council or an Elders-in-Residence experience. Educators and others receive advice on working with Elders, especially in being flexible with requests for their participation such as sending invitations well in advance.

Indigenous peoples can also work with libraries as liaison officers to Native communities.[65] School administrators are asked to appoint a review committee to examine curricular material.[66] The SAA Protocols remind librarians and archivists that the process of consulting may involve communicating with more than one individual and such contact may need to be made more than once.[67] These protocols call on tribal communities to let librarians and archivists know who will serve in the role of cultural community representative. Regardless of the advising structure, the ATSILIRN Protocols recommend that librarians document how they have worked with tribal communities on handling traditional knowledge.[68]

Many of these documents address the roles, needs, and responsibilities of various constituencies impacted by traditional knowl-

[64] Assembly of Alaska Native Educators, *Guidelines for Respecting Cultural Knowledge*, 3.

[65] ATSILIRN, "ATSILIRN Protocols."

[66] Assembly of Alaska Native Educators, *Guidelines for Respecting Cultural Knowledge*, 9.

[67] SAA, "Protocols for Native Archival Materials."

[68] ATSILIRN, "ATSILIRN Protocols."

edge expression. The Mataatua Declaration offers recommendations for indigenous peoples; state, national, and international
agencies; and for the United Nations. The "Guidelines for Respecting Cultural Knowledge" addresses its guidelines to those involved
in education—Native Elders, authors and illustrators, curriculum
developers and administrators, educators, editors and publishers,
document reviewers, researchers, Native language specialists, Native community organizations, and the general public. The SAA
Protocols list guidelines for two interest groups: archives and libraries and Native American communities.

Several of the documents presented here call for the establishment of libraries and/or indigenous library organizations. The
Mataatua Declaration asks Native peoples to "establish international indigenous information centres and networks." The "Guidelines for Respecting Cultural Knowledge" asks curriculum developers and administrators to establish a repository that would hold and
make accessible locally developed curricula.[69]

These and other documents describe the need for continuing
education on these topics and staffing of libraries with Native per-
sonnel. With the Guidelines for Protecting Cultural Knowledge,
the Assembly of Alaska Native Educators suggests that educational
administrators and people who develop classroom curriculum
"Provide an in-depth cultural orientation program for all new
teachers and administrators."[70] Authors and illustrators are called
on to experience a community firsthand before they begin their
writing process. The need for more staff with cultural expertise can
be explained by current workforce demographics: "Although there
has been no census of Indigenous employees, it is clear that no
information organizations employ large numbers and that to date,
the best endeavors of libraries and archives have been little more
than tokenism with Indigenous employees clustered in lower level
positions and one short term contract or trainee terms of employ-

---

[69] Assembly of Alaska Native Educators, *Guidelines for Respecting Cultural Knowledge*, 8.
[70] Ibid., 9.

ment."[71] Simply put, the most logical approach to increasing cultural knowledge may be to "develop the observation and listening skills necessary to acquire an in-depth understanding of the knowledge system indigenous to the local community and apply that understanding."[72]

## Library observance of indigenous protocols

McCook and Phenix remind every librarian to defend human rights: "It is up to the individual librarian to what degree she or he will defend the principles of human rights. In some cases a library's administrators may permit human rights violations but front-line librarians can make brave stands in defense."[73] By building relationships with indigenous communities and among indigenous librarians, seeking out and ordering indigenous literature, and following indigenous protocols, librarians can begin to uphold the principles of human rights in their daily work.

General ALA guidelines serve as protocols for librarianship and lay the foundation for respecting indigenous protocols and for prioritizing cultural rights in librarianship. These protocols are expressed in professionally held beliefs and performance of routine professional tasks. Some of our protocols are also described and promulgated via written documents. For example, the "Guidelines for Behavioral Performance of Reference and Information Service Providers" describes successful behaviors that librarians can employ in answering queries in both face-to-face and remote settings. These behaviors are expressed in a protocol embracing the categories of approachability, interest, listening/inquiring, searching, and follow-up.[74] Librarian-based protocols can be used for educating students, training library staff, and in performance evaluation.

---

[71] ATSILIRN, "ATSILIRN Protocols."

[72] Assembly of Alaska Native Educators, *Guidelines for Respecting Cultural Knowledge*, 10.

[73] Kathleen de la Peña McCook and Katharine J. Phenix, "Public Libraries and Human Rights," *Public Library Quarterly* 25:1/2 (2006): 57-73, 68.

[74] Reference and User Services Association, "Guidelines for Behavioral Performance of Reference and information Service Providers," ALA

Tribal community and librarian community protocol overlap in their support for diversity. Diversity is one of ALA's five key action areas, along with education and continuous learning, equity of access, intellectual freedom, and 21st century literacy.[75] ALA's expression of diversity is reflected in the organization's formal and informal structure, including the existence of an Office for Diversity, the presence of a Diversity Officer within ALA, and the establishment of a Committee on Diversity at the Council or governance level. In addition, ALA's growing commitment to diversity issues include a national student initiative called the Spectrum Scholarship Program that has awarded over 500 scholarships and provided leadership training to students of color from community groups not well represented in the library workforce. Units of ALA also carry forth the Organization's diversity focus. For example, diversity committees within the eleven ALA divisions include the American Association of School Librarians Task Force on Diversity in the Organization, the joint REFORMA and Association for Library Service to Children's Belpré Award Selection Committee, and the Josey Spectrum Scholar Mentor Program of the Association of College and Research Libraries. In addition, there are five ethnic library associations affiliated with ALA, providing their members with opportunities to focus on library services to American Indians, Latinos and the Spanish speaking, African-Americans, Chinese Americans, and Asian and Pacific Islanders.

Some library protocols discuss interpersonal contact with indigenous peoples while others address use of material that contains indigenous content. Examples include:

> * The ATSILIRN Protocols, first written in 1995 and then updated in 2005. The document clearly states that the protocols are intended both "to guide libraries, archives and information services in appropriate ways to interact with Aboriginal and Torres Strait Islander people in the communities which the organiza-

---

http://www.ala.org/ala/mgrps/divs/rusa/resources/guidelines/guidelinesbehavioral.cfm (accessed 3 June 2009).

[75] ALA, "Key Action Areas," *ALA Handbook of Organization* (Chicago: ALA, 2008), 8.

tions serve, and to handle materials with Aboriginal and Torres Strait Islander Content."[76] Such protocols provide guidance on interactions between librarians in Australia and their indigenous peoples and the handling of items on indigenous culture housed in library collections.

* The *Guidelines for Respecting Cultural Knowledge*, released in 2000 by the Assembly of Alaska Native Educators, with representatives from nearly twenty educational and cultural associations. This document describes how stakeholders in education "may increase their cultural responsiveness" through a variety of actions.[77]

* The "Protocols for Native Archival Materials," the result of an SAA-sponsored meeting of indigenous peoples from Australia, Canada, and the United States in 2007. The document presents guidelines in ten content areas including "Building Relationships of Mutual Respect" and "Awareness of Native American Communities and Issues."[78]

For the most part, these documents can be considered as guidelines or suggested behaviors. They call on participants to engage in careful, and sometimes passive, actions through such verbs as participate, help make explicit, make a point, seek out, carefully review, follow, arrange, make every effort, carefully explain, and assist. The SAA Protocols are slightly more pointed: they are guidelines for action. The authors of the ATSILIRN Protocols point out that they are neither prescriptive nor definitive.

The latest contributor to this discussion is the ALA with its draft principles, "Librarianship and Traditional Cultural Expressions: Nurturing Understanding and Respect."[79] In many ways, the principles are an expanded interpretation of Article 27, conjoining

---

[76] ATSILIRN, "ATSILIRN Protocols: The Protocols."

[77] Assembly of Alaska Native Educators, *Guidelines for Respecting Cultural Knowledge*, 4-21.

[78] SAA, "Protocols for Native Archival Materials: The Protocols"

[79] ALA, *Draft Principles, Librarianship and Traditional Cultural Expressions: Nurturing Understanding and Respect* (2009) http://wo.ala.org/tce/ 2009/04/01/draft-of-library-principles-and-tces/ (accessed 5 June 2009).

the concepts of community and cultural property/intellectual rights protection. The Principles introduce the relationship between library services and expressions of traditional cultures, including print and archival resources. Librarians and Native peoples are asked to work together through five sets of roles or areas of activity: meaning and social context; respect, recognition, understanding; responsibility; reciprocity and collaboration; and stewardship.[80] While some may think these principles are in direct opposition of ALA's key value statements, especially those describing equity of access and intellectual freedom, the Principles also speak to the deep-seated professional values of social justice and social responsibility.

## Conclusion

Responding to a look at Article 27, this chapter has begun to outline both the importance of cultural rights of indigenous peoples and the necessary framework for supporting indigenous peoples' cultural life in libraries. In this chapter we call for a collective responsibility informed by responses to Article 27. The omission of indigenous peoples from the UDHR, including in Article 27, has been partially ameliorated by a range of indigenous rights documents. Librarians should thus use the vital concepts of Article 27 not by themselves but as an introduction to an ongoing conversation about cultural rights and human rights policy. The individual rights at the foundations of the UDHR, based in a western free market value system, promote a sense of individual entitlement and a false sense of neutrality. Collective rights, on the other hand, require in response a collective responsibility to see and respond to institutionalized oppression, the systematic economic, social, and cultural oppression of people with a group identity. Reading Article 27 in the context of indigenous documents and for the purpose of informing a practice of library advocacy for marginalized groups is the only way to create libraries and a field of librarianship that actively support diverse cultures.

---

[80] Ibid.

Taking on this collective responsibility requires librarians to turn away from the individualism idealized by some significant threads of the U.S. government and of librarianship, and to support indigenous self-determination of the creation and stewardship of cultural property and practices. This support includes building trust with local communities, learning about and respecting protocols, recruiting indigenous librarians, and sustaining indigenous publishers and authors. Ultimately, respectfully protecting not only access to participation in the cultural life of the community but also participation in the cultural lives of our communities requires taking the lead from indigenous librarians and indigenous library organizations.

Librarianship is making its first tentative steps toward a public membership discussion of the impact of supporting these beliefs on the rights and beliefs of indigenous peoples. One result of this way-finding is the new ALA principle, "Librarianship and Traditional Cultural Expressions: Nurturing Understanding and Respect." This document calls on librarians to consider a different world view, one that values community ownership across time and one that asks librarians to work with tribal communities to assure that content is treated with the interests of these communities in mind.[81] Librarians have addressed and triumphed in the face of change. They have adopted technologies, introduced new services, reached out to all sectors of their communities, and kept their doors open in the midst of natural disaster and budgetary constraints.

In Sweden in 2001, the International Indigenous Librarians' Forum (IILF) published a statement reaffirming indigenous claims to self-determination and control of cultural rights in libraries: "the use of intellectual and cultural property in any medium, especially in light of the global instantaneous impact of the electronic environment, without the approval of all appropriate authorities is unacceptable."[82] At annual meetings of the IILF, librarians continue

---

[81] Ibid.
[82] International Indigenous Librarians' Forum. Compiled by Wendy Sinclair-Sparvier and Hinureina Mangan. "International Indigenous Librari-

to emphasize the importance of indigenous involvement in libraries and in the conference itself as a way of generating "partnerships to create a global network for sharing information, ideas and practices."[83] In individual libraries and at meetings like the IILF, librarians can begin to follow Beardslee's lead and remake libraries as sites of the cultural lives of library communities. Dion calls on nonindigenous Canadians to participate in "learning from" First Nations stories and storytellers which "offer a disruption of Canadians' understanding of themselves," such "learning from" "requires recognition of implication in the relationship and a responsible response that is not easily accomplished."[84] Non-indigenous librarians must reflect on their own implication in the relationship with indigenous peoples and actively share their control over the library space to allow indigenous cultural self-determination.

This recent indigenous activism in librarianship draws on a long history. In his book *Paper Talk: A History of Libraries, Print Culture, and Aboriginal Peoples in Canada before 1960*, Brendan Frederick R. Edwards recounts how indigenous peoples resist(ed) the efforts of missionaries and the government to use "books and libraries as tools to assist them in their efforts to convert, civilise, and assimilate the First Peoples of Canada. Aboriginal peoples, on the other hand, through writing, alphabetic literacy, and the eventual formation of libraries, were taking steps to partially control the construction of their own identities within the contexts of colonialism and Western understandings of knowledge and communication."[85] Considering cultural rights calls librarians to be responsible to this dual history, both acknowledging the employment of libraries in an

---

ans' Forum 1999-2009: Background & Outcomes from Past Fora." "Outcomes," *Sixth International Indigenous Librarians' Forum 2009: Maku Ano e Hanga Toku Nei Whare: Determining Our Future* (November 2008) http://www.trw.org.nz/iilf2009_outcomes.php (accessed 6 November 2009).

[83] Ibid.

[84] Dion, *Braiding Histories*, 58-59.

[85] Brendan Frederick R. Edwards, *Paper Talk: A History of Libraries, Print Culture, and Aboriginal Peoples in Canada before 1960* (Lanham, MD: Scarecrow Press/Rowman & Littlefield, 2005), xv.

attempt to eradicate indigenous cultures and recognizing the resistance and generative indigenous cultural work both in and outside of libraries. Recognizing this intellectual history in her recent chapter "Digging at the Roots: Locating an Ethical, Native Criticism," Lisa Brooks explains the significance of one way of being cultural: "I believe that for us, at this moment, there can be no move more important than establishing that our work, our writing is part of an extensive indigenous intellectual tradition. What we have at stake is not only the recognition of the validity of our knowledge, but the sustenance of indigenous epistemologies."[86] The Declaration on the Rights of Indigenous Peoples in turn recognizes that sustaining cultural life requires active support and intervention; standing back will not work. The Declaration's Article 16, for example, includes the call for states to "take effective measures to ensure that State-owned media duly reflect indigenous cultural diversity." Libraries, as influences on and as a form of state-owned media (broadly interpreted), should be sites for this discussion. Expanding librarians' engagement with human rights discourse strengthens the field of librarianship and makes an argument for the ongoing importance of librarians as theorists of and advocates for social justice.

We are confident that library services will continue to flourish. Their respectful and collaborative involvement with traditional cultural expressions will benefit libraries, patrons, and tribal communities. As the ATSILIRN Protocols point out, "simply being aware and understanding the issues can play a large part in actually making a difference."[87] And, as noted in the SAA Protocols, such relationships of trust must be built over time.

---

[86] Lisa Brooks, "Digging at the Roots: Locating an Ethical, Native Criticism," in *Reasoning Together*, ed. Native Critics Collective (Janice Acoose, Lisa Brooks, Tol Foster, LeAnne Howe, Daniel Heath Justice, Phillip Carroll Morgan, Kimberly Roppolo, Cheryl Suzack, Christopher B. Teuton, Sean Teuton, Robert Warrior, Craig S. Womack), (Norman, OK: University of Oklahoma, 2008), 234-264, 234-235.

[87] ATSILIRN, "ATSILIRN Protocols: Intellectual Property."

# United Nations Declaration of Human Rights

**PREAMBLE**

Whereas recognition of the inherent dignity and of the equal and inalienable rights of all members of the human family is the foundation of freedom, justice and peace in the world,

Whereas disregard and contempt for human rights have resulted in barbarous acts which have outraged the conscience of mankind, and the advent of a world in which human beings shall enjoy freedom of speech and belief and freedom from fear and want has been proclaimed as the highest aspiration of the common people,

Whereas it is essential, if man is not to be compelled to have recourse, as a last resort, to rebellion against tyranny and oppression, that human rights should be protected by the rule of law,

Whereas it is essential to promote the development of friendly relations between nations,

Whereas the peoples of the United Nations have in the Charter reaffirmed their faith in fundamental human rights, in the dignity and worth of the human person and in the equal rights of men and women and have determined to promote social progress and better standards of life in larger freedom,

Whereas Member States have pledged themselves to achieve, in co-operation with the United Nations, the promotion of universal re-

spect for and observance of human rights and fundamental freedoms,

Whereas a common understanding of these rights and freedoms is
of the greatest importance for the full realization of this pledge,

**Now, Therefore THE GENERAL ASSEMBLY proclaims THIS
UNIVERSAL DECLARATION OF HUMAN RIGHTS** as a com-
mon standard of achievement for all peoples and all nations, to the
end that every individual and every organ of society, keeping this
Declaration constantly in mind, shall strive by teaching and education to promote respect for these rights and freedoms and by progressive measures, national and international, to secure their universal and effective recognition and observance, both among the
peoples of Member States themselves and among the peoples of
territories under their jurisdiction.

**Article 1.**

- All human beings are born free and equal in dignity and
  rights. They are endowed with reason and conscience and
  should act towards one another in a spirit of brotherhood.

**Article 2.**

- Everyone is entitled to all the rights and freedoms set forth
  in this Declaration, without distinction of any kind, such as
  race, colour, sex, language, religion, political or other opinion, national or social origin, property, birth or other
  status. Furthermore, no distinction shall be made on the
  basis of the political, jurisdictional or international status
  of the country or territory to which a person belongs,
  whether it be independent, trust, non-self-governing or
  under any other limitation of sovereignty.

**Article 3.**

- Everyone has the right to life, liberty and security of person.

**Article 4.**

- No one shall be held in slavery or servitude; slavery and the slave trade shall be prohibited in all their forms.

**Article 5.**

- No one shall be subjected to torture or to cruel, inhuman or degrading treatment or punishment.

**Article 6.**

- Everyone has the right to recognition everywhere as a person before the law.

**Article 7.**

- All are equal before the law and are entitled without any discrimination to equal protection of the law. All are entitled to equal protection against any discrimination in violation of this Declaration and against any incitement to such discrimination.

**Article 8.**

- Everyone has the right to an effective remedy by the competent national tribunals for acts violating the fundamental rights granted him by the constitution or by law.

**Article 9.**

- No one shall be subjected to arbitrary arrest, detention or exile.

**Article 10.**

* Everyone is entitled in full equality to a fair and public hearing by an independent and impartial tribunal, in the determination of his rights and obligations and of any criminal charge against him.

**Article 11.**

* (1) Everyone charged with a penal offence has the right to be presumed innocent until proved guilty according to law in a public trial at which he has had all the guarantees necessary for his defence.

* (2) No one shall be held guilty of any penal offence on account of any act or omission which did not constitute a penal offence, under national or international law, at the time when it was committed. Nor shall a heavier penalty be imposed than the one that was applicable at the time the penal offence was committed.

**Article 12.**

* No one shall be subjected to arbitrary interference with his privacy, family, home or correspondence, nor to attacks upon his honour and reputation. Everyone has the right to the protection of the law against such interference or attacks.

**Article 13.**

* (1) Everyone has the right to freedom of movement and residence within the borders of each state.

* (2) Everyone has the right to leave any country, including his own, and to return to his country.

**Article 14.**

- (1) Everyone has the right to seek and to enjoy in other countries asylum from persecution.
- (2) This right may not be invoked in the case of prosecutions genuinely arising from non-political crimes or from acts contrary to the purposes and principles of the United Nations.

**Article 15.**

- (1) Everyone has the right to a nationality.
- (2) No one shall be arbitrarily deprived of his nationality nor denied the right to change his nationality.

**Article 16.**

- (1) Men and women of full age, without any limitation due to race, nationality or religion, have the right to marry and to found a family. They are entitled to equal rights as to marriage, during marriage and at its dissolution.
- (2) Marriage shall be entered into only with the free and full consent of the intending spouses.
- (3) The family is the natural and fundamental group unit of society and is entitled to protection by society and the State.

**Article 17.**

- (1) Everyone has the right to own property alone as well as in association with others.
- (2) No one shall be arbitrarily deprived of his property.

**Article 18.**

- Everyone has the right to freedom of thought, conscience and religion; this right includes freedom to change his religion or belief, and freedom, either alone or in community

with others and in public or private, to manifest his religion or belief in teaching, practice, worship and observance.

## Article 19.

- Everyone has the right to freedom of opinion and expression; this right includes freedom to hold opinions without
  interference and to seek, receive and impart information
  and ideas through any media and regardless of frontiers.

## Article 20.

- (1) Everyone has the right to freedom of peaceful assembly and association.
- (2) No one may be compelled to belong to an association.

## Article 21.

- (1) Everyone has the right to take part in the government
  of his country, directly or through freely chosen representatives.
- (2) Everyone has the right of equal access to public service
  in his country.
- (3) The will of the people shall be the basis of the authority
  of government; this will shall be expressed in periodic and
  genuine elections which shall be by universal and equal
  suffrage and shall be held by secret vote or by equivalent
  free voting procedures.

## Article 22.

- Everyone, as a member of society, has the right to social
  security and is entitled to realization, through national effort and international co-operation and in accordance with
  the organization and resources of each State, of the economic, social and cultural rights indispensable for his dignity and the free development of his personality.

**Article 23.**

- (1) Everyone has the right to work, to free choice of employment, to just and favourable conditions of work and to protection against unemployment.
- (2) Everyone, without any discrimination, has the right to equal pay for equal work.
- (3) Everyone who works has the right to just and favourable remuneration ensuring for himself and his family an existence worthy of human dignity, and supplemented, if necessary, by other means of social protection.
- (4) Everyone has the right to form and to join trade unions for the protection of his interests.

**Article 24.**

- Everyone has the right to rest and leisure, including reasonable limitation of working hours and periodic holidays with pay.

**Article 25.**

- (1) Everyone has the right to a standard of living adequate for the health and well-being of himself and of his family, including food, clothing, housing and medical care and necessary social services, and the right to security in the event of unemployment, sickness, disability, widowhood, old age or other lack of livelihood in circumstances beyond his control.
- (2) Motherhood and childhood are entitled to special care and assistance. All children, whether born in or out of wedlock, shall enjoy the same social protection.

**Article 26.**

- (1) Everyone has the right to education. Education shall be free, at least in the elementary and fundamental stages. Elementary education shall be compulsory. Technical and

professional education shall be made generally available
and higher education shall be equally accessible to all on
the basis of merit.
- (2) Education shall be directed to the full development of
the human personality and to the strengthening of respect
for human rights and fundamental freedoms. It shall promote understanding, tolerance and friendship among all
nations, racial or religious groups, and shall further the activities of the United Nations for the maintenance of
peace.
- (3) Parents have a prior right to choose the kind of education that shall be given to their children.

## Article 27.

- (1) Everyone has the right freely to participate in the cultural life of the community, to enjoy the arts and to share
in scientific advancement and its benefits.
- (2) Everyone has the right to the protection of the moral
and material interests resulting from any scientific, literary
or artistic production of which he is the author.

## Article 28.

- Everyone is entitled to a social and international order in
which the rights and freedoms set forth in this Declaration
can be fully realized.

## Article 29.

- (1) Everyone has duties to the community in which alone
the free and full development of his personality is possible.
- (2) In the exercise of his rights and freedoms, everyone
shall be subject only to such limitations as are determined
by law solely for the purpose of securing due recognition
and respect for the rights and freedoms of others and of
meeting the just requirements of morality, public order and
the general welfare in a democratic society.

- (3) These rights and freedoms may in no case be exercised contrary to the purposes and principles of the United Nations.

**Article 30.**

- Nothing in this Declaration may be interpreted as implying for any State, group or person any right to engage in any activity or to perform any act aimed at the destruction of any of the rights and freedoms set forth herein.

# About the Contributors

**Frans Albarillo** is the Instruction Librarian at Hawai'i Pacific University. A graduate of the University of Hawai'i Library and Information Science Program, he also holds a second Master of Arts in Linguistics for his studies in language documentation and conservation. His research interests include library history, human rights and minority rights, language policy, and multicultural library instruction. In his spare time he also likes to write short stories.

**Julie Biando Edwards** is Assistant Professor and Ethnic Studies Librarian & Multicultural Coordinator at the Mansfield Library, University of Montana in Missoula. She has a Master of Arts in English from the University of Connecticut and received her Master of Science in Library and Information Science from the University of Illinois, Urbana-Champaign in 2005. She began her career as a public librarian and has research interests in human rights and librarianship as well as in libraries and community. She is the co-author of "Libraries, Community Life, and Cultural Identity," delivered at the Libraries From a Human Rights Perspective Conference in Ramallah, Palestine, 2008 and "Culture and the New Iraq: The Iraq National Library and Archives, 'Imagined Community,' and the Future of the Iraqi Nation, " published in *Libraries & the Cultural Record*, August 2008.

**Stephan P. Edwards** is a PhD student in Anthropology at The University of Montana and holds Masters degrees in History with an emphasis in Human Rights Studies from the University of Connecticut (2002), and in Cultural Anthropology from Brandeis University (2007). A former Assistant Professor of History and Political Science at Central Wyoming College, where he taught courses on human rights theory and practice, he is currently the Director of First-Year Interest Groups and Adjunct Professor at the University of Montana in Missoula. He is the co-author of "Libraries, Community Life, and Cultural Identity," delivered at the Libraries From a Human Rights Perspective Conference in Ramallah, Palestine, 2008 and "Culture and the New Iraq: The Iraq National Library and Archives, 'Imagined Community,' and the Future of the Iraqi Nation, " published in *Libraries & the Cultural Record*, August 2008.

**Kristen Hogan** is a literary activist writer, teacher, and workshop director based in Austin, Texas. She has worked as a professor of Women's and Gender Studies and as a book buyer and manager at feminist bookstores. Currently a graduate student at the School of Information at the University of Texas at Austin, she believes it is a responsibility of libraries to advocate for diverse literatures and to work against systems of oppression.

**Natalia Taylor Poppeliers** is Assistant Professor and Library Collections Coordinator at the University of South Carolina Aiken. She also serves as Country Specialist on the Central African Republic (C.A.R.) for the human rights organization Amnesty International USA. She has a Master of Arts in Language, Reading, and Culture from the University of Arizona and a Master of Library Science with a specialization in African Studies Librarianship from Indiana University, Bloomington. Additionally, Poppeliers spent three and a half years working in health education, adult literacy, and library development in the C.A.R. with the United States Peace Corps. In addition to cultural rights and libraries, her research interests include: information ethics, human rights, and the role of libraries and archives; information needs of human rights and civil society groups in Central Africa; the open access movement and its impact on scholarship in Sub-Saharan Africa; sustainability measurements for African libraries; impact of violent conflict on information provision; and access to information as a human right.

**Dr. Loriene Roy** is a Professor in the School of Information, the University of Texas at Austin. She is Anishinabe, enrolled on the

White Earth Reservation, a member of the Minnesota Chippewa Tribe. She is Director and Founder of "If I Can Read, I Can Do Anything," a national reading club for Native students. Dr. Roy is the first convener of the Special Interest Group on Indigenous Matters for IFLA, the International Federation of Library Associations.

# Index

www.ingramcontent.com/pod-product-compliance
Lightning Source LLC
Chambersburg PA
CBHW032351280326
41935CB00008B/538